# The Children's Hymnary

*Editors*
Arlene Hartzler and John Gaeddert

*Illustrated by*
Ruth Eitzen

FAITH AND LIFE PRESS
NEWTON, KANSAS

Printed in the United States of America
Library of Congress Catalog Card Number 67-24327


3M1683M1068

# Appreciation

The publication of *The Children's Hymnary* represents the generous labor of many people. To mention all who served as resource persons for a book like this would require a lengthy list. Recognizing that it is difficult to trace where all the helpful suggestions came from, we wish herewith to express our gratitude to all persons who had any part in the formulation of the manuscript.

We gratefully acknowledge special indebtedness to the following:

Marvin Dirks, Sr., Walter Hohmann, Lester Hostetler, William Klassen, Russell Lantz, Harold Moyer, Vernon Neufeld, and George Wiebe who set up guidelines for the project and gave valuable counsel.

James Bixel, Evelyn Bushong, George Wiebe, and Harold Moyer for their arrangements.

Harold Moyer, Orlando Schmidt, and others who assisted in checking the music engraver's copy.

Delphine Martens and Griselda Shelly for clearing copyright permissions and styling of the hymn texts.

Cornelia Lehn, Anneliese Birky, and George Wiebe for guidance and counsel on the German texts which are included.

Ruth Eitzen who prepared the art illustrations.

Authors and composers whose songs are included; to publishing houses and individuals who gave permission to use their material.

Willard Claassen who assumed much of the responsibility for encouraging the editors and for carrying out the many tasks which are part of the publication of such a book.

The friendly cooperation of the many who worked together to make this publication possible is greatly appreciated.

Arlene Hartzler and
John Gaeddert, Editors

# Preface

*The Children's Hymnary* was specially planned for use in Christian education, for children's worship, and for use by families in the home. The hymns come from many countries of the world. Many of them are old, some more recent and contemporary. Three hymns were copyrighted for the first time. Some of the great hymns of the church have been deliberately included so that the strength and virility of our Christian heritage may become part of the experience of our children.

The hymns were selected for use with primary and kindergarten children. Many of the hymns are also appropriate for use with junior-age children. An index in the back of the book classifies hymns for use with various age groups. Hymns for special Sundays and festivals are also listed.

In selecting the hymns for *The Children's Hymnary,* the compilers and editors were guided by principles established by the Worship and Music Committee. The editors were asked to choose hymns with singable tunes, with a proper range for children, use of wholesome imagery, elements of meaningful repetition, and to correlate with the objectives for Christian education. The selection includes carols, folk tunes, and great hymns of the church. The hymns have simple accompaniments; the hymnbook contains original two-color illustrations for children. There are thirteen German texts.

This hymnary contains resources for worship in the form of music, such as table graces, offertories, and prayers. Helpful indexes are found in the back of the book to make the book more useful in a variety of situations. Learn to use it.

Plans for this hymnbook began in 1959. The preparation of *The Children's Hymnary* was guided by the Worship and Music Committee of the Board of Education and Publication. The members of this committee during the period of planning were Marvin Dirks, Sr., John Gaeddert, Walter Hohmann, Lester Hostetler, William Klassen, Russell Lantz, Harold Moyer, Vernon Neufeld, Orlando Schmidt, and George Wiebe.

The editors of *The Children's Hymnary,* Arlene Hartzler and John Gaeddert, gave many months of hard work to the task of compiling and editing the hymns in this book. We owe them a large debt of gratitude.

It is hoped that the publication of this hymnary will improve the worship in church schools and other children's groups, so that the child will be helped to participate meaningfully in the worship of the church.

Willard Claassen

# Contents

# The Hymns

# Sing to God in Joyful Voice

Virginia C. Murdock

Spanish Melody

Sing to God in joy-ful voice, In His lov-ing hand re-joice.

Earth and sky a-like pro-claim Prais-es to His ho-ly name.

He who guides the swal-low's flight Will not lose thee from His sight;

All thy trust in Him con-fide, Ev-er in His love a-bide.

Words from *New Music Horizons*, Book III, © 1953, Silver Burdett Company

His Wonder and Creation

2

# This Is My Father's World

Maltbie D. Babcock

Franklin L. Sheppard

1. This is my Fa - ther's world, And to my lis-tening ears,
2. This is my Fa - ther's world, The birds their car - ols raise,

All na - ture sings, and round me rings The mu - sic of the spheres.
The morn-ing light, the lil - y white, De - clare their Maker's praise.

This is my Fa - ther's world: I rest me in the thought
This is my Fa - ther's world: He shines in all that's fair;

Of rocks and trees, of skies and seas; His hand the won-ders wrought.
In the rustling grass I hear Him pass, He speaks to me ev-ery-where.

His Wonder and Creation

# 3    Can You Count the Stars

Johann Wilhelm Hey, Tr. by H. W. Dulcken
Stanza 2, tr. by Lester Hostetler

German Folk Tune

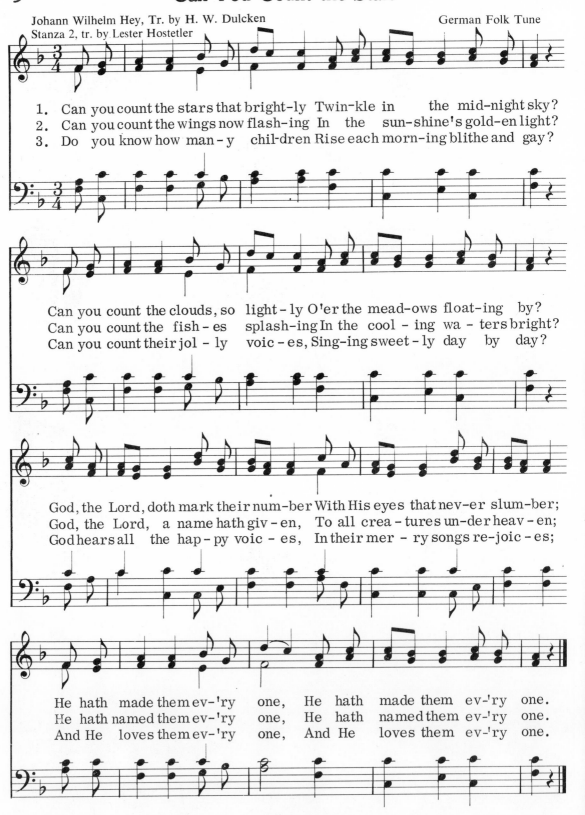

1. Can you count the stars that bright-ly Twin-kle in    the mid-night sky?
2. Can you count the wings now flash-ing In  the  sun-shine's gold-en light?
3. Do  you know how man-y  chil-dren Rise each morn-ing blithe and gay?

Can you count the clouds, so  light - ly O'er the mead-ows float-ing  by?
Can you count the fish - es   splash-ing In  the  cool - ing  wa - ters bright?
Can you count their jol - ly  voic - es, Sing-ing sweet - ly day  by  day?

God, the Lord, doth mark their num-ber With His eyes that nev-er slum-ber;
God, the Lord, a  name hath giv-en, To all crea - tures un-der heav - en;
God hears all  the  hap-py voic - es, In their mer - ry songs re-joic - es;

He hath made them ev-'ry  one,  He hath  made them ev-'ry  one.
He hath named them ev-'ry  one,  He hath  named them ev-'ry  one.
And He  loves them ev-'ry  one,  And He  loves them ev-'ry  one.

His Wonder and Creation

1 Weisst du, wieviel Sternlein stehen an dem blauen Himmelszelt?
Weisst du, wieviel Wolken gehen weithin über alle Welt?
Gott der Herr hat sie gezählet, dass ihm auch nicht eines fehlet
an der ganzen grossen Zahl, an der ganzen grossen Zahl.

2 Weisst du, wieviel Mücklein spielen in der hellen Sonnenglut,
wieviel Fischlein auch sich kühlen in der hellen Wasserflut?
Gott der Herr rief sie mit Namen, dass sie all ins Leben kamen,
dass sie nun so fröhlich sind, dass sie nun so fröhlich sind.

3 Weisst du, wieviel Kinder frühe stehn aus ihren Bettlein auf,
dass sie ohne Sorg und Mühe fröhlich sind im Tageslauf?
Gott im Himmel hat an allen seine Lust, sein Wohlgefallen,
kennt auch dich und hat dich lieb, kennt auch dich und hat dich lieb.

# Who Made the Sky So Bright and Blue 4

Author Unknown

Composer Unknown

1. Who made the sky so bright and blue? Who made the fields so green?
2. Who made the birds to soar so high And taught them how to sing?
3. 'Twas God who made this world so fair, The sun, the sky, the air;

Who made the flow'rs that smell so sweet, In pret - ty col - ors seen?
Who made the pret - ty but - ter - fly And paint - ed her bright wing?
'Twas God who made the sea, the ground, And all the things a - round.

His Wonder and Creation

## 5
# Praise to God for Things We See

Matilda M. Penstrone, alt.

French Folk Song
Arr. and alt. by Roberta Bitgood

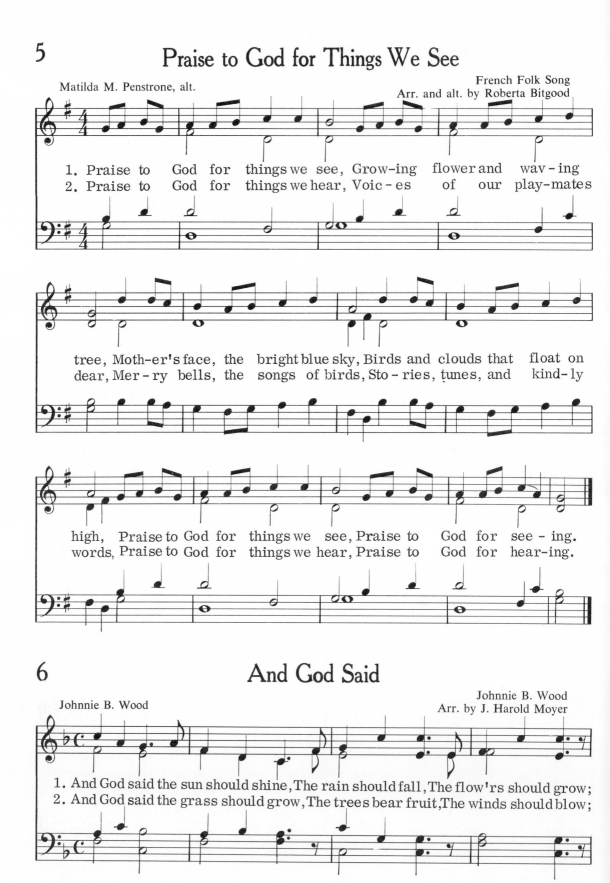

1. Praise to God for things we see, Grow-ing flower and wav-ing
2. Praise to God for things we hear, Voic-es of our play-mates

tree, Moth-er's face, the bright blue sky, Birds and clouds that float on
dear, Mer-ry bells, the songs of birds, Sto-ries, tunes, and kind-ly

high, Praise to God for things we see, Praise to God for see-ing.
words, Praise to God for things we hear, Praise to God for hear-ing.

## 6
# And God Said

Johnnie B. Wood

Johnnie B. Wood
Arr. by J. Harold Moyer

1. And God said the sun should shine, The rain should fall, The flow'rs should grow;
2. And God said the grass should grow, The trees bear fruit, The winds should blow;

His Wonder and Creation

And God said the birds should sing, And it was so, was so.
And God said the streams should flow, And it was so, was so.

## Who Made the Stars

7

Miriam Drury

Miriam Drury

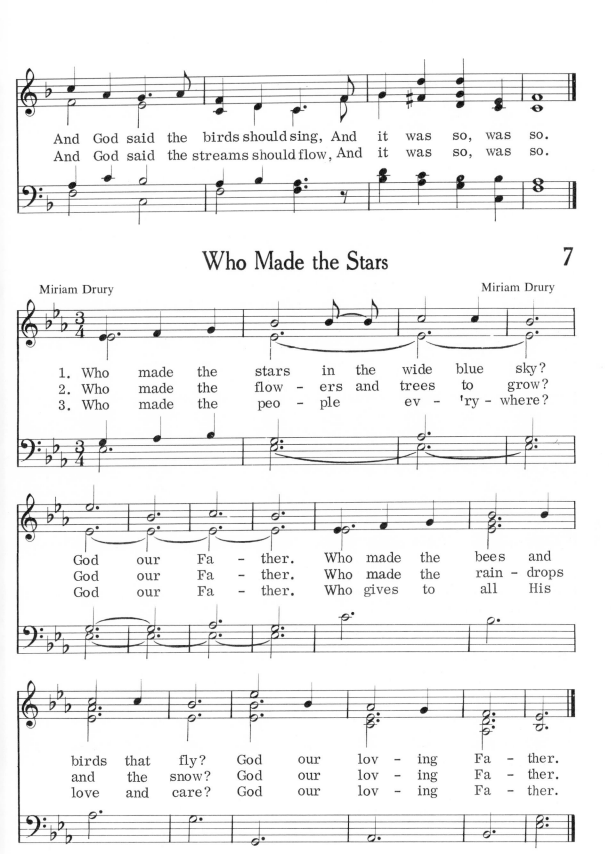

1. Who made the stars in the wide blue sky?
2. Who made the flow - ers and trees to grow?
3. Who made the peo - ple ev - 'ry - where?

God our Fa - ther. Who made the bees and
God our Fa - ther. Who made the rain - drops
God our Fa - ther. Who gives to all His

birds that fly? God our lov - ing Fa - ther.
and the snow? God our lov - ing Fa - ther.
love and care? God our lov - ing Fa - ther.

His Wonder and Creation

8 ## A Little Seed Lay Fast Asleep

Clara Writer

English Traditional May Day Carol, coll. and arr.
by Lucy Broadwood, har. by R. Vaughan Williams

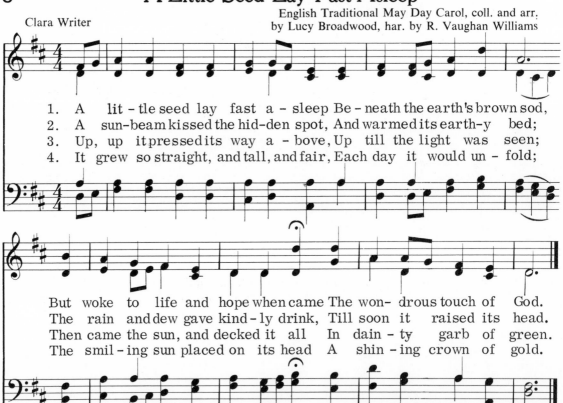

1. A lit-tle seed lay fast a-sleep Be-neath the earth's brown sod,
2. A sun-beam kissed the hid-den spot, And warmed its earth-y bed;
3. Up, up it pressed its way a-bove, Up till the light was seen;
4. It grew so straight, and tall, and fair, Each day it would un-fold;

But woke to life and hope when came The won-drous touch of God.
The rain and dew gave kind-ly drink, Till soon it raised its head.
Then came the sun, and decked it all In dain-ty garb of green.
The smil-ing sun placed on its head A shin-ing crown of gold.

5 At last it stood, with thousands more,
A golden ear of corn,
God's gift to man, our daily food,
From little seedlings born.

6 So children are the seeds God plants
Within His garden fair:
He loves and guards them every day;
They have His constant care.

7 And they may grow so straight and pure,
So good and full of grace;
A crown of gold is theirs, when they
Shall see the Savior's face.

His Wonder and Creation

# Give to Our God Immortal Praise

9

Founded on Psalm 136
Isaac Watts

Melody from *Geistliche Kirchengesänge*

1. Give to our God im-mor-tal praise; Mer-cy and truth are all His ways;
2. Give to the Lord of lords re - nown; The King of kings with glory crown:
3. He built the earth, He spread the sky, And fixed the star-ry lights on high:
4. He fills the sun with morn-ing light, He bids the moon direct the night:
5. Give to our God im-mor-tal praise; Mer-cy and truth are all His ways;

Won - ders of grace to God be -
His mer-cies ev - er shall en -
Hal - le - lu - jah, Hal-le - lu-jah! Won - ders of grace to God be -
His mer-cies ev - er shall en -
Won - ders of grace to God be -

long, Re - peat His mer-cies in your song:
dure, When lords and kings are known no more:
long, Re - peat His mer-cies in your song: Hal-le - lu - jah, Hal-le-
dure, When sun and moon shall shine no more:
long, Re - peat His mer-cies in your song:

lu - jah, Hal-le - lu-jah, Hal-le - lu - jah, Hal-le - lu - jah!

His Wonder and Creation

# 10     For the Beauty of the Earth

Folliott S. Pierpoint

Conrad Kocher

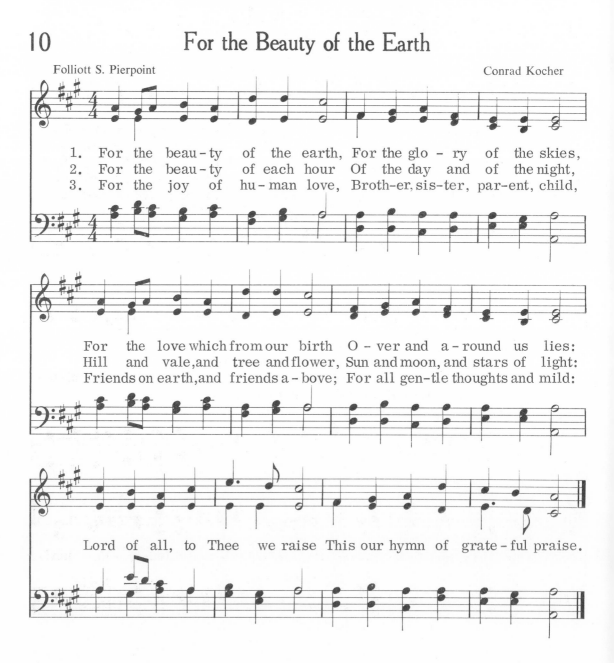

1. For the beau-ty of the earth, For the glo-ry of the skies,
2. For the beau-ty of each hour Of the day and of the night,
3. For the joy of hu-man love, Broth-er, sis-ter, par-ent, child,

For the love which from our birth O-ver and a-round us lies:
Hill and vale, and tree and flower, Sun and moon, and stars of light:
Friends on earth, and friends a-bove; For all gen-tle thoughts and mild:

Lord of all, to Thee we raise This our hymn of grate-ful praise.

His Wonder and Creation

# All Things Bright and Beautiful

Cecil Frances Alexander

Danish Folk Song

1. Each lit - tle flower that o - pens, Each lit - tle bird that sings,
2. The pur - ple - head - ed moun - tain, The riv - er run - ning by,
3. The cold winds in the win - ter, The pleas - ant sum - mer sun,
4. He gave us eyes to see them, And lips that we might tell

God made their glow - ing col - ors, He made their ti - ny wings.
The sun - set and the morn - ing red That bright - en up the sky.
The ripe fruits in the gar - den, He made them ev - ery one.
The good - ness of the Fa - ther Who do - eth all things well.

Yes, all things bright and beau - ti - ful, All crea - tures great and small,

And all things wise and won - der - ful, The Lord God made them all.

His Wonder and Creation

# 12     I Sing the Mighty Power of God

Isaac Watts

*Gesangbuch der Herzogl.*
*Wirtembergischen Katholischen Hofkapelle*

1. I sing the might-y power of God, That made the mountains rise;
2. I sing the good-ness of the Lord, That filled the earth with food;
3. There's not a plant or flower be-low, But makes Thy glories known;

That spread the flow-ing seas a-broad, And built the loft-y skies.
He formed the crea-tures with His word, And then pro-nounced them good.
And clouds a - rise, and tem-pests blow, By or - der from Thy throne;

I sing the Wis-dom that or-dained The sun to rule the day;
Lord, how Thy won-ders are dis-played, Wher-e'er I turn my eye:
While all that bor-rows life from Thee Is ev - er in Thy care,

The moon shines full at His command, And all the stars o - bey.
If I sur - vey the ground I tread, Or gaze up-on the sky!
And ev - 'ry-where that man can be, Thou, God, art pres-ent there.

His Might and Power

# The God of Abraham Praise

Daniel ben Judah
Tr. by Thomas Olivers

Hebrew Melody
Arr. by Meyer Leoni

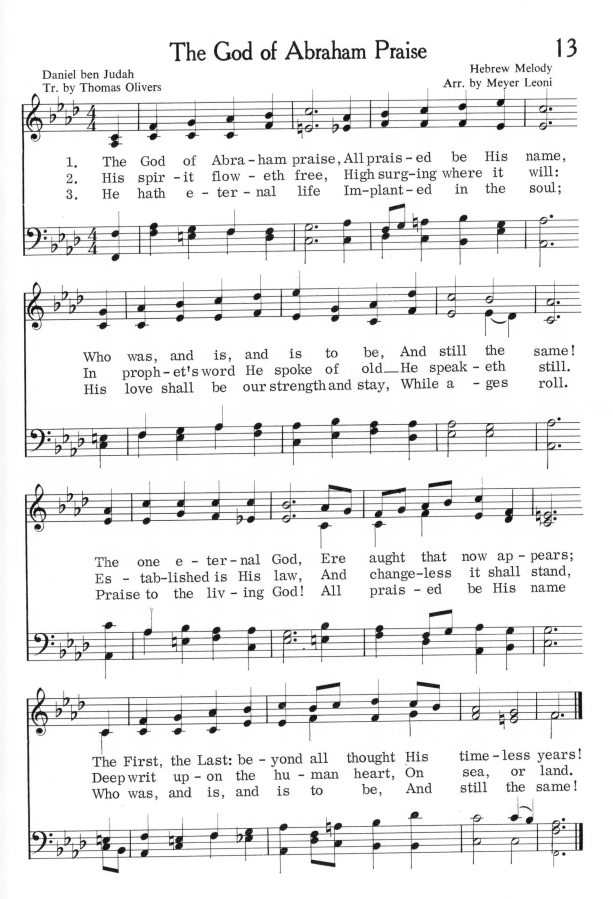

1. The God of Abra-ham praise, All prais-ed be His name,
2. His spir-it flow-eth free, High surg-ing where it will:
3. He hath e-ter-nal life Im-plant-ed in the soul;

Who was, and is, and is to be, And still the same!
In proph-et's word He spoke of old—He speak-eth still.
His love shall be our strength and stay, While a-ges roll.

The one e-ter-nal God, Ere aught that now ap-pears;
Es-tab-lished is His law, And change-less it shall stand,
Praise to the liv-ing God! All prais-ed be His name

The First, the Last: be-yond all thought His time-less years!
Deep writ up-on the hu-man heart, On sea, or land.
Who was, and is, and is to be, And still the same!

His Might and Power

# 14 Before the Lord We Bow

F. S. Key

John Darwall

1. Be - fore the Lord we bow, The God who reigns a - bove,
2. The na - tion Thou hast blest May well Thy love de - clare,
3. May ev - 'ry moun - tain height, Each vale and for - est green,

And rules the world be - low In bound-less pow'r and love;
From foes and fears at rest, Pro-tect - ed by Thy care;
Shine in Thy Word's pure light, And its rich fruits be seen;

Our thanks we bring In joy and praise;
Still let it be Thy fixed a - bode;
May ev - 'ry tongue Be tuned to praise,

Our hearts we raise To heav'n's high King.
Be Thou our God, Thy peo - ple we.
And join to raise A grate - ful song.

His Might and Power

# Come, Thou Almighty King

Charles Wesley

Felice de Giardini

1. Come, Thou al - might - y King, Help us Thy
2. Come, Thou in - car - nate Word, Gird on Thy
3. Come, ho - ly Com - fort - er, Thy sa - cred
4. To the great One in Three E - ter - nal

name to sing, Help us to praise: Fa - ther, all -
might - y sword, Our prayer at - tend: Come, and Thy
wit - ness bear In this glad hour: Thou who al -
prais - es be Hence ev - er-more. His sov-ereign

glo - ri - ous, O'er all vic - to - ri - ous, Come, and reign
peo - ple bless, And give Thy word suc-cess; Spir - it of
might - y art, Now rule in ev - 'ry heart, And ne'er from
maj - es - ty May we in glo - ry see And to e -

o - ver us, An - cient of Days.
ho - li - ness On us de - scend.
us de - part, Spir - it of power.
ter - ni - ty, Love and a - dore.

His Might and Power

# 16     O Worship the King, All Glorious Above

Robert Grant

Arr. from J. Michael Haydn

1. O wor-ship the King, all glo-rious a-bove,
2. O tell of His might, O sing of His grace,
3. Thy boun-ti-ful care, what tongue can re-cite?
4. Frail chil-dren of dust, and fee-ble as frail,

O grate-ful-ly sing His power and His love;
Whose robe is the light, whose can-o-py space;
It breathes in the air, it shines in the light;
In Thee do we trust, nor find Thee to fail;

Our Shield and De-fend-er, the An-cient of Days,
His char-iots of wrath the deep thun-der-clouds form,
It streams from the hills, it de-scends to the plain,
Thy mer-cies how ten-der, how firm to the end,

Pa-vil-ioned in splen-dor, and gird-ed with praise.
And dark is His path on the wings of the storm.
And sweet-ly dis-tils in the dew and the rain.
Our Ma-ker, De-fend-er, Re-deem-er, and Friend!

His Might and Power

# God, Whose Name Is Love

**17**

Florence Hoatson

Composer Unknown
Arr. by Paul G. Bunjes

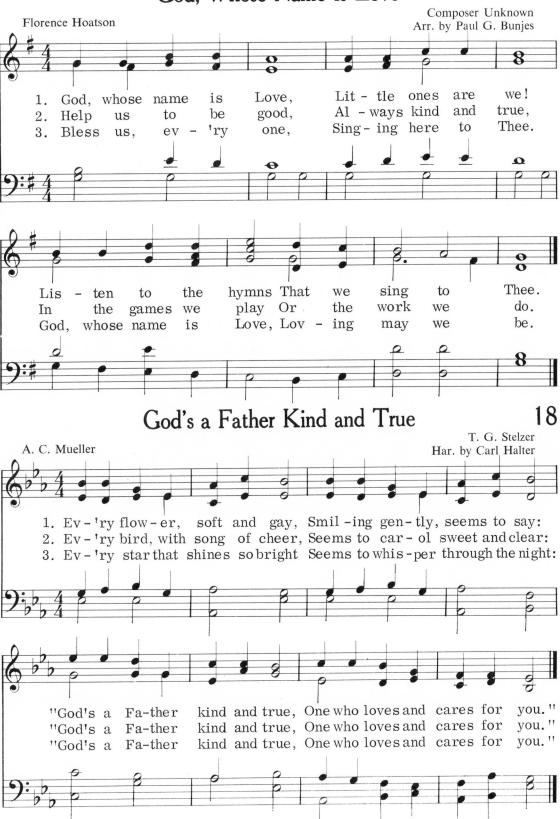

1. God, whose name is Love, Lit - tle ones are we!
2. Help us to be good, Al - ways kind and true,
3. Bless us, ev - 'ry one, Sing - ing here to Thee.

Lis - ten to the hymns That we sing to Thee.
In the games we play Or the work we do.
God, whose name is Love, Lov - ing may we be.

# God's a Father Kind and True

**18**

A. C. Mueller

T. G. Stelzer
Har. by Carl Halter

1. Ev - 'ry flow - er, soft and gay, Smil - ing gen - tly, seems to say:
2. Ev - 'ry bird, with song of cheer, Seems to car - ol sweet and clear:
3. Ev - 'ry star that shines so bright Seems to whis - per through the night:

"God's a Fa - ther kind and true, One who loves and cares for you."
"God's a Fa - ther kind and true, One who loves and cares for you."
"God's a Fa - ther kind and true, One who loves and cares for you."

His Love and Care

**19**

# I Love God's Tiny Creatures

George Wallace Briggs

Gordon Slater

1. I love God's ti - ny crea-tures That wan-der wild and free,
2. Dear Fa-ther, who hast all things made, And carest for them all,

The cor - al-coat-ed la - dy-bird, The vel - vet humming bee;
There's none too great for Thy great love, Nor an - y-thing too small:

Shy lit - tle flow-ers in hedge and dyke; That hide themselves a - way;
If Thou canst spend such ten - der care On things that grow so wild,

God paints them, though they are so small, God makes them bright and gay.
How won - der-ful Thy love must be For me, Thy lov - ing child.

His Love and Care

# God Is the Loving Father

Mabel Niedermeyer

Finnish Folk Song
Arr. by Roberta Bitgood

1. God is the lov-ing Fa-ther Of chil-dren ev-'ry-where; No
2. He loves all those in far lands Whom I may nev-er see; He

mat-ter where their homes are, They live with-in His care.
al-so loves the chil-dren Who live next door to me.

I'm glad God is the Fa-ther of chil-dren ev-'ry-where, And

that we all may love Him and talk with Him in prayer.

His Love and Care

**21**

# I Love to Think That Jesus Saw

Ada Skemp

Walford Davies 1869-1941

1. I love to think that Je-sus saw The same bright sun that shines to-day;
2. The same white moon with sil-ver face That sails a-cross the sky at night,
3. The same great God that hears my prayers Heard His, when Jesus knelt to pray;

It gave Him light to do His work, And smiled up-on His play.
He used to see in Gal-i-lee, And watch it with de-light.
He is my Fa-ther, who will keep His child through ev-ery day.

**22**

# Teach Us, Dear Lord, to Pray

GREENE

Calvin W. Laufer

Edward Shippen Barnes

1. Teach us, dear Lord, to pray, To trust Thee as we should;
2. Thy love sur-rounds us all With con-stant, pa-tient care;

And help us feel that, come what may, Thy gifts are al-ways good.
Thy ten-der heart, be-fore we call, A-waits our ear-nest prayer.

His Love and Care

# The Lord's My Shepherd

23

Psalm 23
Francis Rous

Jane S. Irvine

1. The Lord's my Shep - herd, I'll not want; He makes me
2. My soul He doth re - store a - gain, And me to
3. Yea, though I walk in death's dark vale, Yet will I
4. My ta - ble Thou hast fur - nish - ed In pres - ence
5. Good - ness and mer - cy all my life Shall sure - ly

down to lie In pas - tures green; He lead - eth
walk doth make With - in the paths of right - eous -
fear no ill; For Thou art with me, and Thy
of my foes: My head Thou dost with oil a -
fol - low me, And in God's house for - ev - er -

me The qui - et wa - ters by.
ness, E'en for His own name's sake.
rod And staff me com - fort still.
noint, And my cup o - ver - flows.
more My dwell - ing place shall be.

His Love and Care

# Gentle Jesus, Meek and Mild

Author Unknown

Martin Shaw

Gen-tle Je-sus, meek and mild, Look on me a lit-tle child;

Help me, if it be Thy will; To re-cov-er from all ill.

25

# God Who Made the Earth

Sarah B. Rhodes

Donald S. Barrows, alt.

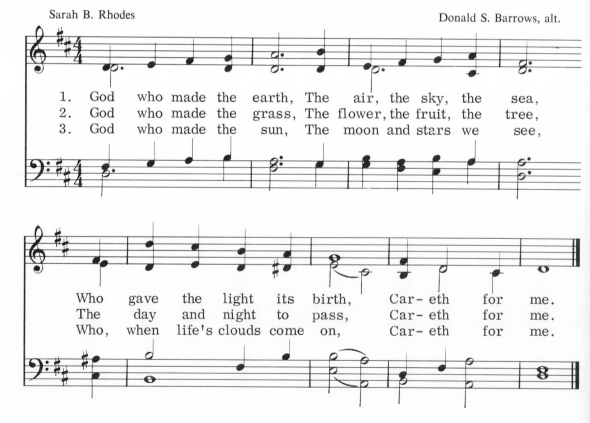

1. God who made the earth, The air, the sky, the sea,
2. God who made the grass, The flower, the fruit, the tree,
3. God who made the sun, The moon and stars we see,

Who gave the light its birth, Car-eth for me.
The day and night to pass, Car-eth for me.
Who, when life's clouds come on, Car-eth for me.

His Love and Care

# God Sees the Little Sparrow Fall

Maria Straub

S. W. Straub

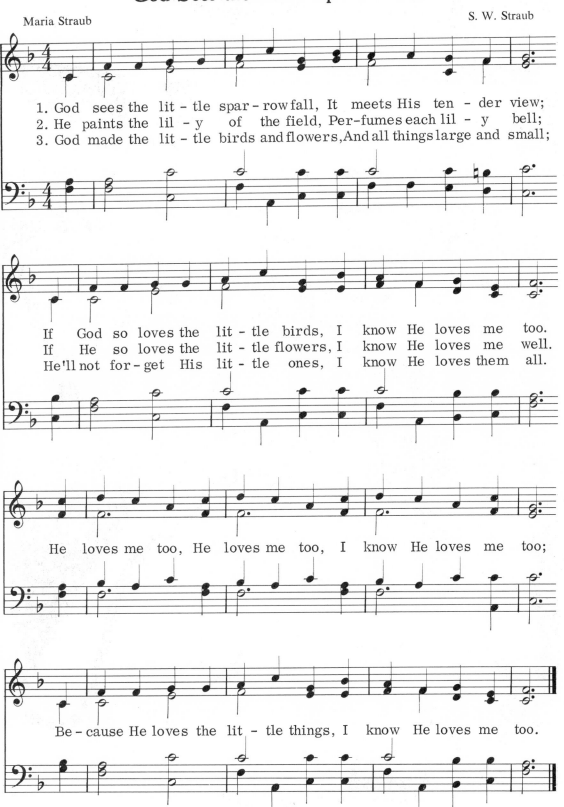

1. God sees the lit - tle spar - row fall, It meets His ten - der view;
2. He paints the lil - y of the field, Per - fumes each lil - y bell;
3. God made the lit - tle birds and flowers, And all things large and small;

If God so loves the lit - tle birds, I know He loves me too.
If He so loves the lit - tle flowers, I know He loves me well.
He'll not for - get His lit - tle ones, I know He loves them all.

He loves me too, He loves me too, I know He loves me too;

Be - cause He loves the lit - tle things, I know He loves me too.

His Love and Care

# O Come, O Come Emmanuel

27

From Latin, 12th century; Stanza 1 tr. by John
Mason Neale; Stanzas 2 and 3 tr. by Henry S. Coffin

13th century Plain Song
Arr. by J. Harold Moyer

1. O come, O come, Em-man-u-el, And ran-som cap-tive Is-ra-el, That mourns in lone-ly ex-ile here, Un-til the Son of God ap-pear. Re-joice! Re-joice! Em-man-u-el Shall come to thee, O Is-ra-el!
2. O come, Thou Wisdom from on high, And or-der all things far and nigh; To us the path of know-ledge show, And cause us in her ways to go. Re-joice! Re-joice! Em-
3. O come, De-sire of na-tions, bind All peo-ples in one heart and mind; Bid en-vy, strife, and quar-rels cease; Fill all the world with heav-en's peace. Re-joice! Re-joice! Em-

His Advent

## 28     On Jordan's Bank the Baptist's Cry

Charles Coffin; Stanzas 1-3 tr. by John
Chandler; Stanzas 4, 5 tr. by unknown

Praetorius
Arr. by Healey Willan

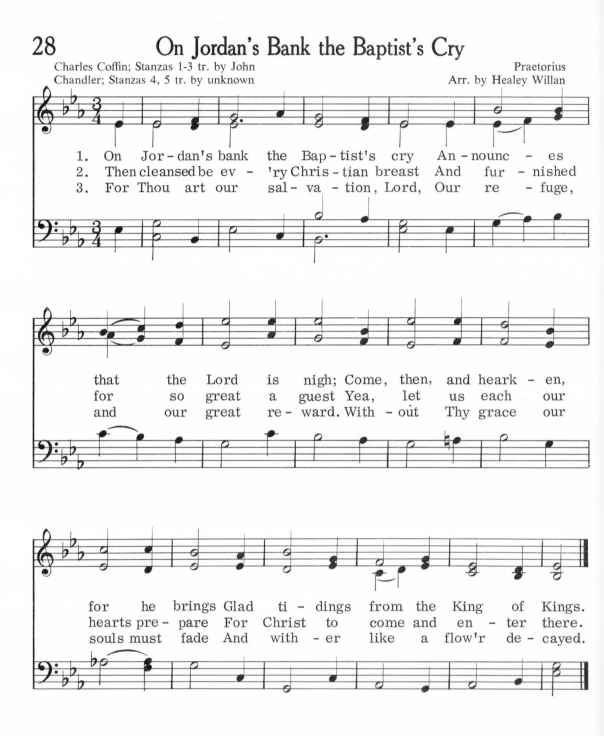

1. On Jor - dan's bank the Bap - tist's cry An - nounc - es
2. Then cleansed be ev - 'ry Chris - tian breast And fur - nished
3. For Thou art our sal - va - tion, Lord, Our re - fuge,

that the Lord is nigh; Come, then, and heark - en,
for so great a guest Yea, let us each our
and our great re - ward. With - out Thy grace our

for he brings Glad ti - dings from the King of Kings.
hearts pre - pare For Christ to come and en - ter there.
souls must fade And with - er like a flow'r de - cayed.

4 Lay on the sick Thy healing hand
And make the fallen strong to stand;
Show us the glory of Thy face
Till beauty springs in every place.

5 All praise, eternal Son, to Thee
Whose advent sets Thy people free,
Whom, with the Father, we adore,
And Holy Ghost forevermore.

His Advent

# O Come, All Ye Faithful

29

Latin Hymn, 18th century
Tr. by Frederick Oakeley

Wade's *Cantus Diversi*

1. O come, all ye faith-ful, joy-ful and tri-um-phant, O
2. Sing, choirs of an-gels, sing in ex-ul-ta-tion, O
3. Yea, Lord, we greet Thee, born this hap-py morn-ing, O

come ye, O come ye to Beth-le-hem! Come and be-hold Him,
sing, all ye cit-izens of heaven a-bove! Glo-ry to God, all
Je-sus, to Thee be all glo-ry given; Word of the Fa-ther,

born the King of an-gels:
glo-ry in the high-est: O come, let us a-dore Him, O
now in flesh ap-pear-ing:

come, let us a-dore Him, O come, let us a-dore Him, Christ, the Lord!

His Birth

## 30      From Heaven Above to Earth I Come

Martin Luther
Tr. by Catherine Winkworth

Valontin Schumann's *Geistliche Lieder*

1. From heaven a - bove to earth I come To bear good
2. To you, this night, is born a child Of Ma - ry,
3. He brings those bless - ings, long a - go Pre - pared by
4. These are the to - kens ye shall mark, The swad - dling

news to ev - 'ry home; Glad ti - dings of great
cho - sen moth - er mild; This lit - tle child, of
God for all be - low; Hence - forth His king - dom
clothes and man - ger dark; There shall ye find the

joy I bring, Where - of I now will say and sing:
low - ly birth, Shall be the joy of all the earth.
o - pen stands To you, as to the an - gel bands.
young child laid, By whom the heavens and earth were made.

His Birth

# O du fröhliche

Johannes Daniel Falk
Tr. by Lester Hostetler

Sicilian Folk Tune

1. O thou joy - ful O thou bless - ed Grace re-veal-ing
2. O thou joy - ful, O thou bless - ed Grace re-veal-ing
3. O thou joy - ful, O thou bless - ed Grace re-veal-ing

Christ-mas - tide! Earth lost in dark-est night, Christ is born, the
Christ-mas - tide! Christ now ap-pear - ing, Our sal-va - tion
Christ-mas - tide! Heav-en-ly hosts are sing-ing, Songs of prais-es

Light of Light. Sing ye, Re - joice ye, On ev -'ry side!
near - ing: Sing ye, Re - joice ye, On ev -'ry side!
ring - ing, Sing ye, Re - joice ye, On ev -'ry side!

1  O du fröhliche,
   o du selige,
   gnadenbringende Weihnachtszeit!
   Welt ging verloren,
   Christ ist geboren:
   freue, freue dich, o Christenheit!

2  O du fröhliche,
   o du selige,
   gnadenbringende Weihnachtszeit!
   Christ ist erschienen,
   uns zu versühnen:
   freue, freue dich, o Christenheit!

3  O du fröhliche,
   o du selige,
   gnadenbringende Weihnachtszeit!
   Himmlische Heere
   jauchzen dir Ehre.
   Freue, freue dich, o Christenheit!

His Birth

## 32      Once in Royal David's City

Cecil Frances Alexander

H. W. Gauntlett
Arr. by Healey Willan

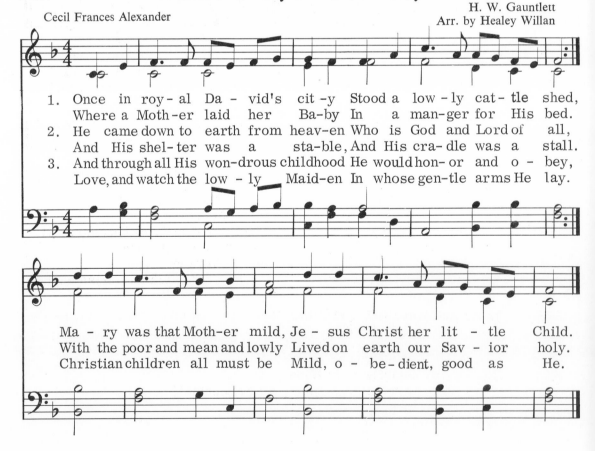

1. Once in roy-al Da-vid's cit-y Stood a low-ly cat-tle shed,
Where a Moth-er laid her Ba-by In a man-ger for His bed.
2. He came down to earth from heav-en Who is God and Lord of all,
And His shel-ter was a sta-ble, And His cra-dle was a stall.
3. And through all His won-drous childhood He would hon-or and o-bey,
Love, and watch the low-ly Maid-en In whose gen-tle arms He lay.

Ma-ry was that Moth-er mild, Je-sus Christ her lit-tle Child.
With the poor and mean and lowly Lived on earth our Sav-ior holy.
Christian children all must be Mild, o-be-dient, good as He.

His Birth

# O Little Town of Bethlehem

Phillips Brooks

Lewis H. Redner

1. O little town of Bethlehem! How still we see thee lie!
2. For Christ is born of Mary, And gathered all above,
3. How silently, how silently, The wondrous gift is giv'n!
4. O holy Child of Bethlehem! Descend to us, we pray;

Above thy deep and dreamless sleep The silent stars go by;
While mortals sleep, the angels keep Their watch of wond'ring love.
So God imparts to human hearts The blessings of His heav'n.
Cast out our sin, and enter in; Be born in us today,

Yet in thy dark streets shineth The everlasting Light;
O morning stars, together Proclaim the holy birth!
No ear may hear His coming, But in this world of sin,
We hear the Christmas angels The great glad tidings tell;

The hopes and fears of all the years Are met in thee tonight.
And praises sing to God the King, And peace to men on earth.
Where meek souls will receive Him still, The dear Christ enters in.
O come to us, abide with us, Our Lord Emmanuel.

His Birth

# Jesus, Born in Bethlea

American Folk Song
From the Southern Highlands

Traditional

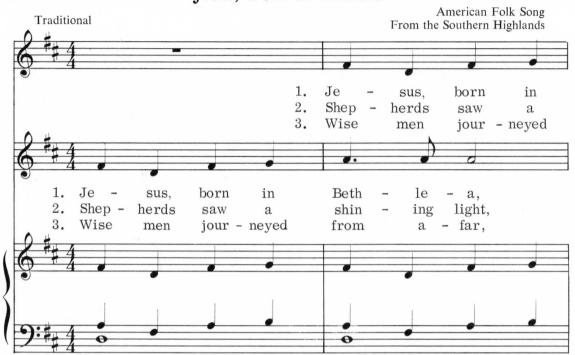

1. Je - sus, born in Beth - le - a,
2. Shep - herds saw a shin - ing light,
3. Wise men jour - neyed from a - far,

Beth - le - a, Je - sus, born in Beth - le - a,
shin - ing light Shep-herds saw a shin - ing light,
from a - far, Wise men jour - neyed from a - far,

Je - sus, born in Beth - le - a, Je - sus, born in
Shep - herds saw a shin - ing light, Shep-herds saw a
Wise men jour - neyed from a - far, Wise men jour - neyed

His Birth

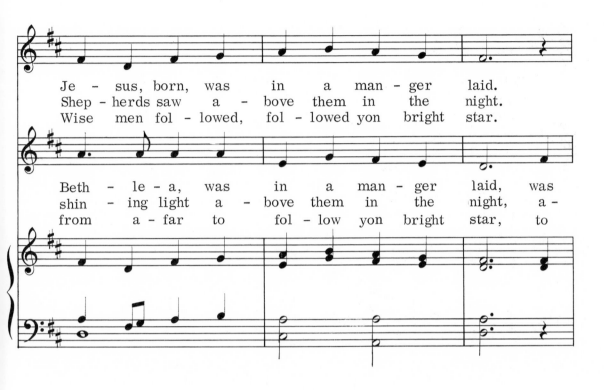

Je - sus, born, was in a man - ger laid.
Shep - herds saw a - bove them in the night.
Wise men fol - lowed, fol - lowed yon bright star.

Beth - le - a, was in a man - ger laid, was
shin - ing light a - bove them in the night, a -
from a - far to fol - low yon bright star, to

Je - sus, born in
Shep - herds saw a
Wise men jour - neyed

in a man - ger laid was
bove them in the night, a -
fol - low yon bright star, to

His Birth

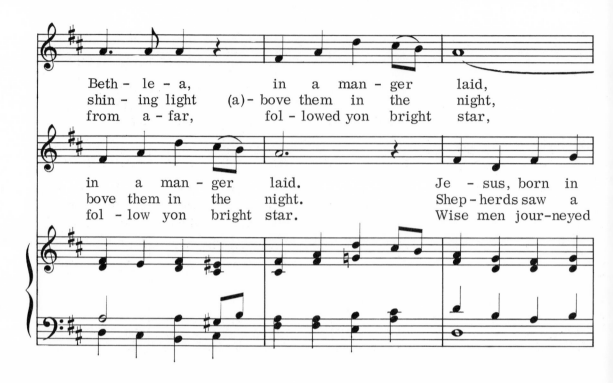

Beth - le - a,                    in a man - ger   laid,
shin - ing light  (a)- bove them  in   the      night,
from  a - far,        fol - lowed yon  bright  star,

in   a man - ger   laid.                    Je - sus, born in
bove them  in   the      night.             Shep - herds saw a
fol - low yon  bright  star.                Wise men jour-neyed

was       in    a   man - ger    laid.
a -   bove them  in   the      night.
and    fol - lowed yon  bright   star.

Beth - le -  a,  was    in   a   man - ger    laid.
shin - ing light  a -  bove them  in   the      night.
from   a - far  to   fol - low  yon  bright    star.

His Birth

# Away in a Manger

Ascribed to Martin Luther

Ascribed to Carl Mueller

1. A - way in a man - ger, no crib for His bed,
2. The cat - tle are low - ing, the poor Ba - by wakes,
3. Be near me, Lord Je - sus; I ask Thee to stay

The lit - tle Lord Je - sus laid down His sweet head,
But lit - tle Lord Je - sus, no cry - ing He makes,
Close by me for - ev - er, and love me I pray.

The stars in the sky looked down where He lay,
I love Thee, Lord Je - sus, look down from the sky,
Bless all the dear chil - dren in Thy ten - der care

The lit - tle Lord Je - sus, a - sleep on the hay.
And stay by my side un - til morn - ing is nigh.
And fit us for heav - en to live with Thee there.

His Birth

# We've Been Told a Joyful Thing

Translated from the French by J. O'Connor, alt.

Besancon Noel

1. We've been told a joy-ful thing, News for all the na-tions.
2. Up and get you quick-ly there, Folk of field and vil-lage!

An-gels have been heard to sing Round the shep-herd sta-tions,
O-ver to that sta-ble bare, Up be-yond the till-age

One in-toned the Glo-ri-a, O-thers, Al-le-lu-i-a.
There you'll find a Ba-by born, With his moth-er in the morn,

Peace on earth, good will to men; War no more the world shall fill.
Sing to-geth-er Glo-ri-a! Sing your Al-le-lu-i-a!

His Birth

# The First Courier

Kate Patton Flenniken

English Folk Melody

1. I'd love to be a shep-herd boy to-night, Un-
2. And when I saw that won - drous light, And
3. I'd fol - low to the man - ger, where The

der the o-pen sky: I'd herd my sheep,and then I'd watch The
heard the an-gels' song, I'd hast-en in-to Beth-le-hem Be-
lit-tle Je-sus lay: I'd drop my crook and wal-let down, So

shin - ing stars go by, The shin-ing stars go by.
hind the shin - ing throng, Be - hind the shin - ing throng.
I could kneel and pray, So I could kneel and pray.

4 But I would have no gift that I
  Could offer to a King,
  Since just a bit of fish and bread
  Was all I had to bring.

5 But I would speed with flying feet
  To wake that sleeping town,
  And lead them to the manger, where
  The new born babe was found.

6 And then we'd hurry in to kneel
  Upon the sanded floor,
  While overhead the great white star
  Lit up the stable door.

His Birth

# As Joseph Was A-walking

R. R. Terry
Arr. by Healey Willan

Traditional

As Jo-seph was a - walk - ing, He heard an an-gel sing; "This night shall be born ———— Our heav - en - ly King.

1. He nei - ther shall be born In hous - en nor in hall,
2. He nei - ther shall be clothed In pur - ple nor in pall,
3. He nei - ther shall be rocked In sil - ver nor in gold,
4. Then be ye glad, good peo - ple, This night of all the year,

His Birth

Nor in the place of Par - a - dise, But in an ox's
But all in fair lin - en As wear the ba - bies
But in a wood - en cra - dle That rocks up - on the
And light you up your can - dles, His star now shin - eth

stall." No - el, No - el.
all." No - el, No - el.
mould." No - el, No - el.
clear." No - el, No - el.

## Shepherds Leave the Hillside

39

Author Unknown

Composer Unknown

Shep-herds leave the hill - side And their wool - ly sheep.

In a crib they find him, Je - sus, fast a - sleep!

His Birth

# 40

# On a Winter Morning

Tr. by Susanna Myers

French Carol
Arr. by James W. Bixel

1. Once to Beth-l'hem shepherds came On a win - ter morn -ing,
2. So we make our gifts to -day, On a win - ter morn -ing,

There to kneel be - fore the Child As the day was dawn-ing.
Think - ing of the Christ Child dear Born on Christ-mas morn-ing.

One had brought a lit - tle lamb, One, a wool - ly
For the ones we love the best, And for those who

sheep - skin warm, With love they came their gifts to bring For the
have the least, In love we give our gifts to - day, In __

His Birth

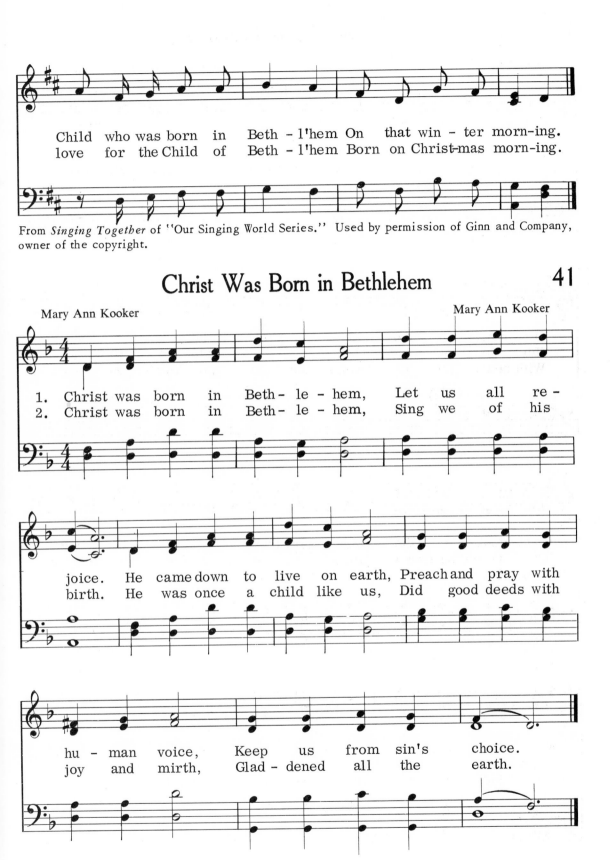

Child who was born in Beth - l'hem On that win - ter morn - ing.
love for the Child of Beth - l'hem Born on Christ-mas morn - ing.

## Christ Was Born in Bethlehem 41

Mary Ann Kooker                                    Mary Ann Kooker

1. Christ was born in Beth - le - hem, Let us all re -
2. Christ was born in Beth - le - hem, Sing we of his

joice. He came down to live on earth, Preach and pray with
birth. He was once a child like us, Did good deeds with

hu - man voice, Keep us from sin's choice.
joy and mirth, Glad - dened all the earth.

His Birth

# O Come, Little Children

Christian von Schmid

Johann A. P. Schulz
Arr. by Laura P. MacCarteney, alt.

1. O come, lit - tle chil - dren, O come, one and all!
2. O see where He's ly - ing, the heav - en - ly boy!
3. O bow with the shep - herds on low bend - ed knee,

O come to the cra - dle in Beth - le - hem's stall!
Here Jo - seph and Ma - ry be - hold Him with joy;
With hearts full of thanks for the gift which you see!

Come, look in the man - ger! there sleeps on the hay,
The shep - herds have come, and are kneel - ing in prayer,
Come, lift up your voi - ces the child to a - dore!

An In - fant so love - ly, in light bright as day.
While songs of the an - gels float o - ver Him there.
Sing joy to the world, love and peace ev - er - more!

His Birth

# Die Kinder an der Krippe

1 Ihr Kinderlein, kommet, o kommet doch all
zur Krippe her, kommet in Bethlehems Stall,
und seht, was in dieser hochheiligen Nacht
der Vater im Himmel für Freude uns macht.

2 O seht in der Krippe im nächtlichen Stall,
seht hier bei der Lichtlein hellglänzendem Strahl,
in reinlichen Windeln das himmlische Kind,
viel schöner und holder als Engel es sind.

3 O beugt, wie die Hirten, anbetend die Knie,
erhebet die Händlein und danket, wie sie!
Stimmt freudig, ihr Kinder, wer sollt sich nicht freun?
stimmt freudig zum Jubel der Engel mit ein.

## Christmas Bells Ring Out Glad News 43

Berdella Blosser Miller
Three-part round

Berdella Blosser Miller

Christ - mas bells ring out glad news,

Christ is born in Beth - le - hem!

Ding dong, ding dong.

His Birth

## 44 As Each Happy Christmas

Johann Wilhelm Hey
Tr. by Harriet R. Spaeth

Friedrich Silcher

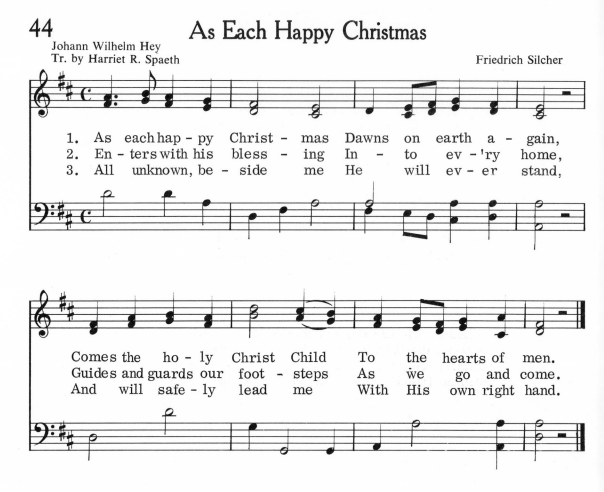

1. As each hap - py Christ - mas Dawns on earth a - gain,
2. En - ters with his bless - ing In - to ev - 'ry home,
3. All unknown, be - side me He will ev - er stand,

Comes the ho - ly Christ Child To the hearts of men.
Guides and guards our foot - steps As we go and come.
And will safe - ly lead me With His own right hand.

## Alle Jahre wieder

1 Alle Jahre wieder
  kommt das Christuskind
  auf die Erde nieder
  wo wir Menschen sind.

2 Kehrt mit seinem Segen
  ein in jedes Haus,
  geht auf allen Wegen
  mit uns ein und aus.

3 Ist auch mir zur Seite
  still und unerkannt,
  das es treu mich leite
  an der lieben Hand.

His Birth

# Silent Night! Holy Night!

Joseph Mohr
Tr. Unknown

Franz Gruber

1. Si - lent night! Ho - ly night! All is calm, all is bright,
2. Si - lent night! Ho - ly night! Shep-herds quake at the sight;
3. Si - lent night! Ho - ly night! Son of God, love's pure light

Round yon Vir - gin Moth - er and Child. Ho - ly In - fant, so
Glo - ries stream from heav - en a - far, Heav-'nly hosts sing, Al -
Ra - diant beams from Thy ho - ly face, With the dawn of re -

ten - der and mild, Sleep in heav-en-ly peace, Sleep in heav-en-ly peace.
le - lu - ia, Christ, the Savior is born! Christ, the Savior is born.
deem - ing grace, Je - sus, Lord, at Thy birth, Je - sus, Lord, at Thy birth.

1 Stille Nacht, heilige Nacht!
Alles schläft, einsam wacht
nur das fromme so selige Paar,
das im Stalle zu Bethlehem war
bei dem himmlischen Kind,
bei dem himmlischen Kind.

2 Stille Nacht, heilige Nacht!
Hirten wird's kund gemacht;
durch der Engel Hallelujah
tönt es laut von ferne und nah:
Jesus, der Retter, ist da,
Jesus, der Retter, ist da.

3 Stille Nacht, heilige Nacht!
Gottes Sohn! — o wie lacht
Lieb' aus deinem holdseligen Mund,
da uns schläget die rettende Stund,
Christ, in deiner Geburt,
Christ, in deiner Geburt.

His Birth

# We Three Kings of Orient Are

John H. Hopkins

John H. Hopkins

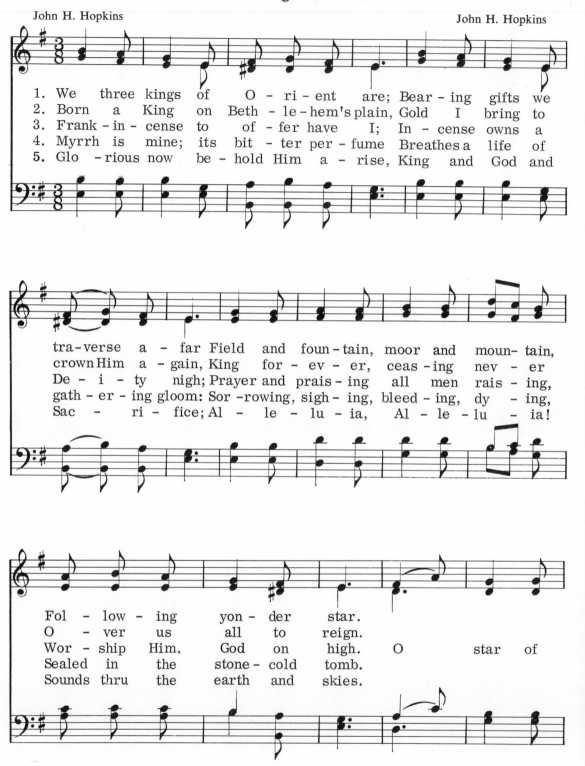

1. We three kings of O - ri - ent are; Bear - ing gifts we
2. Born a King on Beth - le - hem's plain, Gold I bring to
3. Frank - in - cense to of - fer have I; In - cense owns a
4. Myrrh is mine; its bit - ter per - fume Breathes a life of
5. Glo - rious now be - hold Him a - rise, King and God and

tra - verse a - far Field and foun - tain, moor and moun - tain,
crown Him a - gain, King for - ev - er, ceas - ing nev - er
De - i - ty nigh; Prayer and prais - ing all men rais - ing,
gath - er - ing gloom: Sor - rowing, sigh - ing, bleed - ing, dy - ing,
Sac - ri - fice; Al - le - lu - ia, Al - le - lu - ia!

Fol - low - ing yon - der star.
O - ver us all to reign.
Wor - ship Him, God on high. O star of
Sealed in the stone - cold tomb.
Sounds thru the earth and skies.

His Birth

won-der, star of night, Star with roy-al beau-ty bright, West-ward

lead-ing, still pro-ceed-ing, Guide us To Thy per-fect light.

His Birth

**47**

# The Friendly Beasts

Robert Davis, alt.

Medieval French Melody
Attributed to Pierre de Corbeil

1. Je - sus our Broth-er, strong and good, Was hum - bly
2. I, said the don - key, shag-gy and brown, I car-ried His
3. I, said the cow, all white and red, I gave Him my
4. I, said the sheep, with cur - ly horn, I gave Him my

born in a sta - ble rude, And the friend - ly beasts a -
moth-er up hill and down, I car-ried her safe-ly to
man - ger for His bed, I gave Him my hay to
wool for His blan - ket warm, He wore my coat on

round Him stood, Je - sus our Broth-er, strong and good.
Beth-le-hem town; I, said the don - key, shag-gy and brown.
pil - low His head; I, said the cow, all white and red.
Christ - mas morn; I, said the sheep, with cur - ly horn.

5 I, said the dove, from the rafters high,
I cooed Him to sleep that He should not cry,
We cooed Him to sleep, my mate and I;
I, said the dove, from the rafters high.

6 Every beast, by some good spell,
In the stable dark was glad to tell
Of the gift he gave Immanuel;
The gift he gave Immanuel.

His Birth

# O Sing a Song of Bethlehem

Louis F. Benson

Gottfried W. Fink

1. O sing a song of Beth - le - hem, Of shepherds watch - ing there,
2. O sing a song of Naz - a - reth, Of sun - ny days of joy,
3. O sing a song of Gal - i - lee, Of lake and woods and hill,
4. O sing a song of Cal - va - ry, Its glo - ry and dis-may;

And of the news that came to them From an - gels in the air:
O sing of fra - grant flow-ers' breath, And of the sin - less Boy:
Of Him who walked up - on the sea And bade its waves be still:
Of Him who hung up - on the tree And took our sins a - way:

The light that shone on Beth - le - hem Fills all the world to - day;
For now the flowers of Naz - a-reth In ev - 'ry heart may grow;
For though, like waves on Gal - i - lee, Dark seas of trou - ble roll,
For He who died on Cal - va - ry Is ris - en from the grave,

Of Je - sus' birth and peace on earth The an - gels sing al - way.
Now spreads the fame of His dear name On all the winds that blow.
When faith has heard the Mas - ter's word, Falls peace up - on the soul.
And Christ, our Lord, by heav'n a - dored, Is might - y now to save.

His Life and Ministry

49 We Would See Jesus

J. Edgar Park

Lowell Mason

1. We would see Je - sus, lo! His star is shin - ing
2. We would see Je - sus, Ma - ry's son most ho - ly,
3. We would see Je - sus, on the moun - tain teach - ing,

A - bove the sta - ble while the an - gels sing;
Light of the vil - lage life from day to day;
With all the lis - tening peo - ple gath-ered round;

There in a man - ger on the hay re - clin - ing,
Shin - ing re - vealed thro' ev - 'ry task most low - ly,
While birds and flowers and sky a - bove are preach - ing,

Haste, let us lay our gifts be - fore the King.
The Christ of God, the Life, the Truth, the Way.
The bless-ed - ness which sim - ple trust has found.

His Life and Ministry

4 We would see Jesus, in His work of healing,
   At eventide before the sun was set;
   Divine and human, in His deep revealing,
   Of God and man in loving service met.

5 We would see Jesus, in the early morning
   Still as of old He calleth, "Follow Me";
   Let us arise, all meaner service scorning,
   Lord, we are Thine, we give ourselves to Thee!

# Thy Works of Love 50

Calvin W. Laufer

*Scottish Psalter*

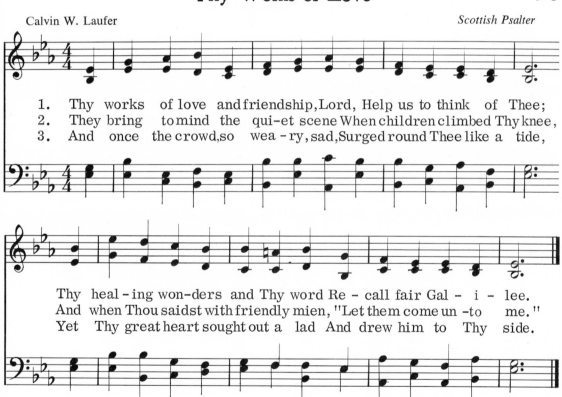

1. Thy works of love and friendship, Lord, Help us to think of Thee;
2. They bring to mind the qui-et scene When children climbed Thy knee,
3. And once the crowd, so wea-ry, sad, Surged round Thee like a tide,

Thy heal-ing won-ders and Thy word Re - call fair Gal - i - lee.
And when Thou saidst with friendly mien, "Let them come un -to me."
Yet Thy great heart sought out a lad And drew him to Thy side.

4 In village, market place, and throng,
   The children cheered Thy days;
   And in the Temple court their song
   To Thee was perfect praise.

5 We love Thee for Thy works divine,
   Still more for what Thou art;
   And that our lives may be like Thine,
   We give Thee, Lord, our hearts.

His Life and Ministry

# At Work Beside His Father's Bench

English Traditional Melody, coll. and arr. by
Lucy Broadwood, har. by R. Vaughan Williams

Alice M. Pullen

1. At work be-side His fa-ther's bench At play when work was done;
2. And in the lit-tle flat-roofed house He served with will-ing hand;
3. Thro' hard-ships and thro' dan-gers too, Un-daunt-ed, tire-less, brave;

In qui-et Gal-i-lee He lived, The friend of ev-'ry one.
His moth-er's dai-ly bur-dens bore, Her joys and plea-sures planned.
For trou-bled, sick, and wea-ry friends His dai-ly life he gave.

Com-rade of boys and girls like us, Play-mate so straight and true,
And as He grew to be a man, He wan-dered far and wide,
And when He left his faith-ful friends, To do His work and will,

In all our work, in all our play, Make us true comrades, too.
To be a friend to ev-'ry one Through-out the coun-try-side.
He prom-ised them He'd be, un-seen, Their faith-ful Com-rade still.

His Life and Ministry

# Far Away in Old Judea

Walter John Mathams

Carey Bonner

1. Far a-way in old Ju - de - a, Lived the gen - tle
2. Through the fields He of - ten led them, Where the love - ly
3. Won-drous sto - ries Je - sus told them Of our Fa - ther's

Lord of love; Hap - py chil - dren gath - ered round Him,
lil - ies grew, Where the crest - ed lark went sing - ing
thought - ful care; How He loves us, leads us, keeps us,

Where - so - ev - er He might move, And they some - times
Up - ward to the sky so blue; Thus with Him and
Ev - 'ry day and ev - 'ry - where; So we nev - er

left their play, Just to fol - low Him all day.
birds and flowers, Glad they spent the gold - en hours.
need to fear, Since His help is al - ways near.

His Life and Ministry

# Once Upon a Hillside

Calvin W. Laufer

Calvin W. Laufer

1. Once up - on a hill - side, Crowds had come to hear
2. Joy - ful - ly they lis-tened, Seat - ed in the grass,
3. Far from home and hun - gry At the close of day,
4. Then with loaves and fish - es, Giv - en by a boy,
5. O we want to thank Him For His love and care!

Je - sus tell the peo - ple God was ver - y near.
And had soon for - got - ten How the glad hours pass.
Just be - cause He loved them Je - sus bade them stay.
Lov - ing- ly He fed them, Sent them home with joy.
For He loves all peo - ple Here and ev - 'ry - where.

His Life and Ministry

# Lonesome Valley

Collected by Gladys Jameson

White Spiritual from the Southern Highlands, U.S.A.

1. Je - sus walk'd this lone-some val - ley, He had to
2. We must walk this lone-some val - ley, We have to
3. You must go and stand your trial, You have to

1. Je - sus walk'd this lone - some val - ley,
3. You must go and stand your tri - al,

walk it by him - self, Oh, no-bod-y else could
walk it by our - selves, Oh no-bod-y else can
stand it by your - self, Oh, no-bod-y else can

Had to walk it by him - self, Oh, no one else
Have to stand it by your - self, Oh, no one else

walk it for Him, He had to walk it by him - self.
walk it for us, We have to walk it by our - selves.
stand it for you. You have to stand it by your-self.

could walk it for Him, Had to walk it by him-self.
can stand it for you. Have to stand it for your-self.

Stanza two may be sung in unison.

His Life and Ministry

# O Master Workman of the Race

Jay T. Stocking

From W. Gawler's *Hymns and Psalms*

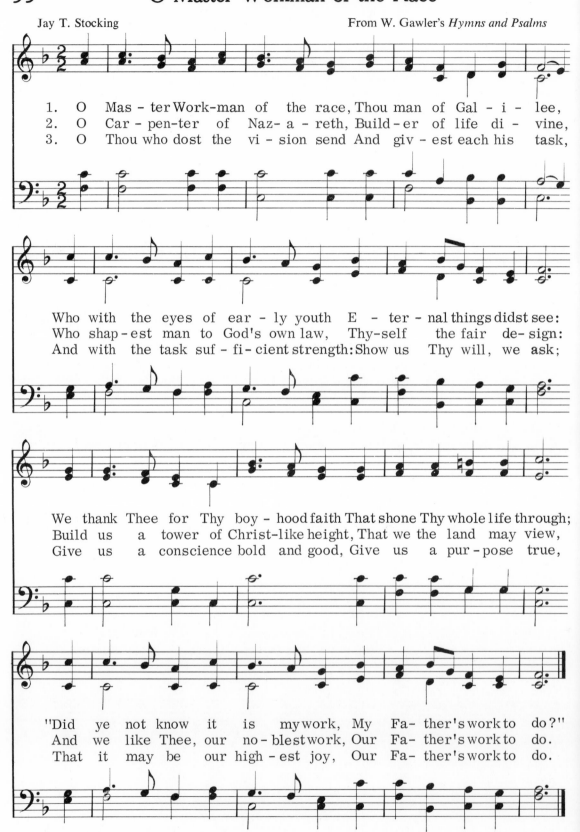

1. O Mas - ter Work-man of the race, Thou man of Gal - i - lee,
2. O Car - pen-ter of Naz - a - reth, Build - er of life di - vine,
3. O Thou who dost the vi - sion send And giv - est each his task,

Who with the eyes of ear - ly youth E - ter - nal things didst see:
Who shap - est man to God's own law, Thy - self the fair de - sign:
And with the task suf - fi - cient strength: Show us Thy will, we ask;

We thank Thee for Thy boy - hood faith That shone Thy whole life through;
Build us a tower of Christ-like height, That we the land may view,
Give us a conscience bold and good, Give us a pur - pose true,

"Did ye not know it is my work, My Fa - ther's work to do?"
And we like Thee, our no - blest work, Our Fa - ther's work to do.
That it may be our high - est joy, Our Fa - ther's work to do.

His Life and Ministry

# All Glory, Laud, and Honor

Theodulph of Orleans
Tr. by John Mason Neale

Melchior Teschner

1. All glo - ry, laud, and hon - or To Thee, Re-deem - er, King,
2. Thou didst ac - cept their prais - es; Ac - cept the prayers we bring,

To whom the lips of chil - dren Made sweet ho - san-nas ring.
Who in all good de - light - est, Thou good and gra - cious King.

The peo - ple of the He - brews With palms before Thee went;
All glo - ry, laud, and hon - or To Thee, Redeem - er King,

Our praise and prayer and an - thems Be - fore Thee we pre-sent.
To whom the lips of chil - dren Made sweet ho - san - nas ring.

His Triumphal Entry

# Hosanna, Loud Hosanna

Jeannette Threlfall

*Hymnal of the Wirtemberg Court Chapel*

1. Ho - san - na, loud ho - san - na The lit - tle chil - dren sang:
2. From Ol - i - vet they fol - lowed 'Mid an ex - ult - ant crowd,
3. "Ho - san - na in the high - est!" That an - cient song we sing,

Through pil - lared court and tem - ple The joy - ful an - them rang;
The vic - tor palm - branch wav - ing, And chant - ing clear and loud;
For Christ is our Re - deem - er, The Lord of heaven our King.

To Je - sus, who had blessed them Close fold - ed to His breast,
The Lord of men and an - gels Rode on in low - ly state,
O may we ev - er praise Him With heart and life and voice,

The chil - dren sang their prais - es, The sim - plest and the best.
Nor scorned that lit - tle chil - dren Should on His bid - ding wait.
And in His bliss - ful pres - ence E - ter - nal - ly re - joice!

His Triumphal Entry

# There Is a Green Hill Far Away

Cecil Frances Alexander

John H. Gower

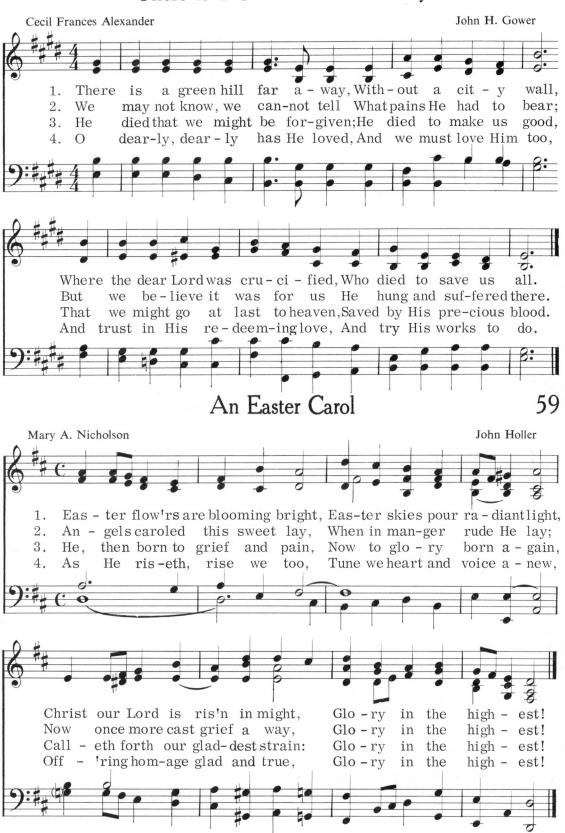

1. There is a green hill far a-way, With-out a cit-y wall,
2. We may not know, we can-not tell What pains He had to bear;
3. He died that we might be for-given; He died to make us good,
4. O dear-ly, dear-ly has He loved, And we must love Him too,

Where the dear Lord was cru-ci-fied, Who died to save us all.
But we be-lieve it was for us He hung and suf-fered there.
That we might go at last to heaven, Saved by His pre-cious blood.
And trust in His re-deem-ing love, And try His works to do.

# An Easter Carol

59

Mary A. Nicholson

John Holler

1. Eas-ter flow'rs are blooming bright, Eas-ter skies pour ra-diant light,
2. An-gels caroled this sweet lay, When in man-ger rude He lay;
3. He, then born to grief and pain, Now to glo-ry born a-gain,
4. As He ris-eth, rise we too, Tune we heart and voice a-new,

Christ our Lord is ris'n in might, Glo-ry in the high-est!
Now once more cast grief a-way, Glo-ry in the high-est!
Call-eth forth our glad-dest strain: Glo-ry in the high-est!
Off-'ring hom-age glad and true, Glo-ry in the high-est!

His Suffering, Death, and Resurrection

# 60 We Welcome Glad Easter

Author Unknown

Welsh Hymn Melody

1. We wel - come glad Eas - ter when Je - sus a - rose
2. And tell how three Ma - rys came ear - ly that day
3. And sing of the an - gel who said: "Do not fear!
4. So think of the prom - ise which Je - sus did give,

And won a great vic - to - ry o - ver His foes.
And there at the tomb found the stone rolled a - way.
Your Sav - ior is ris'n a - gain; He is not here."
That he who be - lieves in Him al - so shall live.

Then raise your glad voic - es, ye chil - dren, and sing,
Then raise your glad voic - es, ye chil - dren, and sing,
Then raise your glad voic - es, ye chil - dren, and sing,
Then raise your glad voic - es, ye chil - dren, and sing,

Bring sweet Eas - ter prais - es to Je - sus, our King.
Bring sweet Eas - ter prais - es to Je - sus, our King.
Bring sweet Eas - ter prais - es to Je - sus, our King.
Bring sweet Eas - ter prais - es to Je - sus, our King.

His Resurrection

# Easter Time

Laura Elizabeth Richards

B. J. Hancock

1. The lit-tle flow'rs came through the ground, At Easter time, at Eas-ter time,
2. The pure white lil - y raised its cup, At Eas-ter time, at Eas-ter time,
3. 'Twas long and long and long a-go, At Eas-ter time, at Eas-ter time,

They raised their heads and looked a-round, At hap-py Eas-ter-time:
The cro - cus to the sky looked up, At hap-py Eas-ter-time:
But still the pure white lil - ies blow, At hap-py Eas-ter-time:

And ev - 'ry lit-tle flower did say,"Good peo-ple bless this ho -ly day,
"We'll hear the song of love," they say,"Its glo-ry shines on us to-day,
And still the lit-tle flower doth say,"Good peo-ple bless this ho -ly day,

For Christ is risen, the an - gels say, At hap-py Eas-ter-time."
O may it shine on us al -way, At hap-py Eas-ter-time."
For Christ is risen, the an - gels say, At hap-py Eas-ter-time."

His Resurrection

## 62 Jesus Christ Is Risen Today

Based on the Latin, 14th century
Stanza 4, Charles Wesley

From *Lyra Davidica*

1. Je - sus Christ is ris'n to - day,   Al - le - lu - ia!
2. Hymns of praise then let us sing   Al - le - lu - ia!
3. But the pains which He en - dured,   Al - le - lu - ia!
4. Sing we to our God a - bove   Al - le - lu - ia!

Our tri - um-phant ho - ly day,   Al - le - lu - ia!
Un - to Christ, our heav'n-ly King,   Al - le - lu - ia!
Our sal - va - tion have pro - cured,   Al - le - lu - ia!
Praise e - ter - nal as His love;   Al - le - lu - ia!

Who did once up - on the cross,   Al - le - lu - ia!
Who en - dured the cross and grave,   Al - le - lu - ia!
Now a - bove the sky He's King,   Al - le - lu - ia!
Praise Him, all ye heav'n - ly host,   Al - le - lu - ia!

Suf - fer to re - deem our loss.   Al - le - lu - ia!
Sin - ners to re - deem and save.   Al - le - lu - ia!
Where the an - gels ev - er sing.   Al - le - lu - ia!
Fa - ther, Son, and Ho - ly Ghost.   Al - le - lu - ia!

His Resurrection

# Christ Is Risen

63

Jeana A. Graham

Katherine Y. Guess

Christ is ris-en, we re - joice! And sing al - le - lu -

ia! With our heart, With our voice, We sing al - le - lu - ia!

May the glo - ry of His love Shine on us from up a - bove.

From *Cherub Hymns,* Harold Flammer, Inc., used by permission.

His Resurrection

**64**

# At the Dawn of Easter Day

Ruth Heller

Old Easter Chorale
Arr. by J. Harold Moyer

1. At the dawn of Eas-ter day The an-gels rolled the rock a - way.
2. To His friends the Lord did come, He brought them joy and blessed each one.

Those who thought the Lord was dead Found He was a - live in - stead.
Told them He would al - ways stay. Thank you, God, for Eas - ter day!

**65**

# Joyful Easter

A. M. Milner-Barry

Old Cornish Carol

1. It is the joy - ful Eas-ter time, Let all sing Hal - le - lu - jah!
2. The church is bright with flowers gay And all Christ's people praise and pray

The merry bells ring out their chime, "But now hath Christ a - ris - en."
For Je-sus rose on Eas - ter Day; Sing joy-ful Hal - le - lu - jah!

His Resurrection

# Come, O Children, Sing to Jesus

F. Smith

*Psalmodia Sacra*
Arr. by Healey Willan

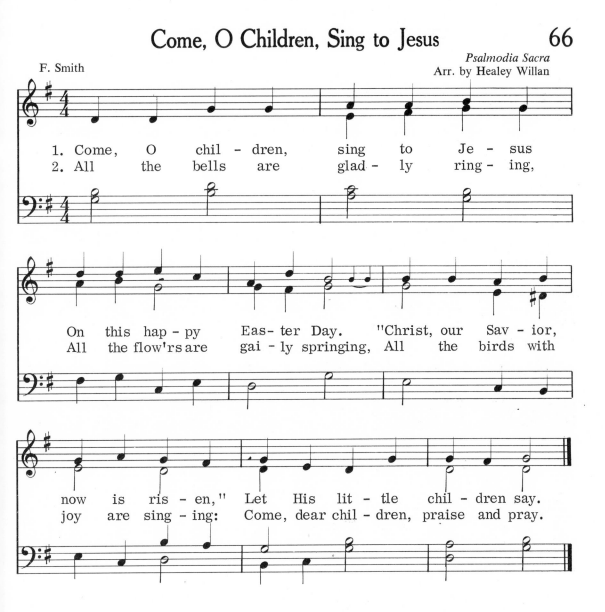

1. Come, O chil-dren, sing to Je-sus
2. All the bells are glad-ly ring-ing,

On this hap-py Eas-ter Day. "Christ, our Sav-ior,
All the flow'rs are gai-ly springing, All the birds with

now is ris-en," Let His lit-tle chil-dren say.
joy are sing-ing: Come, dear chil-dren, praise and pray.

# Christ the Lord Is Risen Today; Alleluia!

Author Unknown

Robert Williams

1. Christ the Lord is ris'n to-day: Al - le-lu - ia!
2. Chris-tians, praise the Lord and say: Al - le-lu - ia!

His Resurrection

**68** # The Church of God Is Everywhere

Nancy Byrd Turner

Old English Melody

1. The church of God is ev - 'ry - where, A shel - ter
2. The church of God is safe and sure. 'Tis built of

and a home; it stands In all the world more firm and
love and faith and prayer; Its doors are ev - er o - pened

strong Than an - y build - ing made with hands. No storm can
wide, And all who will may en - ter there. On hill and

shake the roof or wall, And in it there is room for all.
plain, from shore to shore, A home, a shel - ter, ev - er - more!

God's People

# Glorious Things of Thee Are Spoken

John Newton

Joseph Haydn

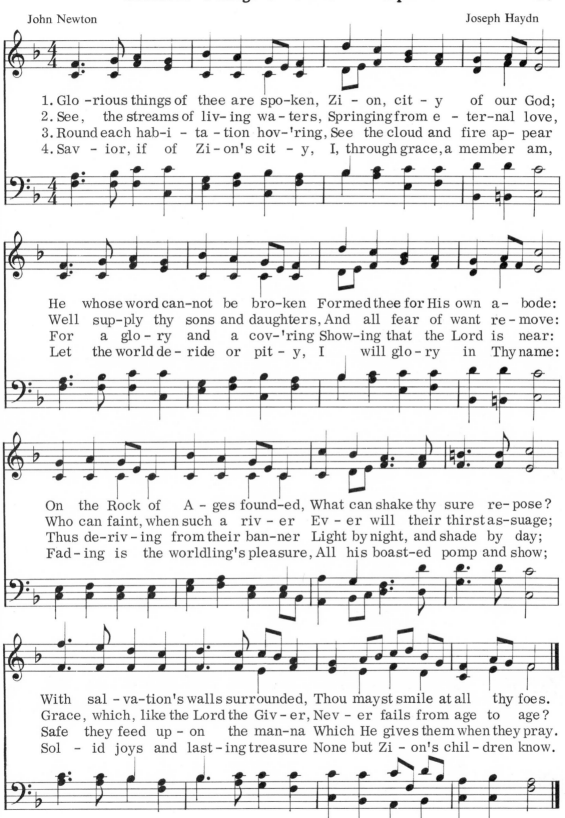

1. Glo -rious things of thee are spo-ken, Zi - on, cit - y  of our God;
2. See,  the streams of liv-ing wa-ters, Springing from e - ter-nal love,
3. Round each hab-i - ta-tion hov-'ring, See the cloud and fire ap- pear
4. Sav - ior, if of Zi-on's cit - y, I, through grace, a member am,

He  whose word can-not be bro-ken Formed thee for His own a- bode:
Well  sup-ply thy sons and daughters, And  all fear of want re - move:
For  a glo - ry  and  a cov'-ring Show-ing that the Lord is  near:
Let  the world de - ride or pit - y, I  will glo-ry  in  Thy name:

On  the Rock of  A - ges found-ed, What can shake thy sure re- pose?
Who can faint, when such a riv - er Ev - er will  their thirst as-suage;
Thus de-riv-ing from their ban-ner Light by night, and shade by  day;
Fad-ing is  the worldling's pleasure, All  his boast-ed pomp and show;

With  sal - va-tion's walls surrounded, Thou mayst smile at all  thy foes.
Grace, which, like the Lord the Giv-er, Nev - er fails from age to  age?
Safe  they feed up - on  the man-na Which He gives them when they pray.
Sol - id joys and last-ing treasure None but Zi - on's chil - dren know.

God's People

## 70 Faith of Our Fathers, Living Still

Frederick W. Faber

Henry F. Hemy and J. G. Walton

1. Faith of our fa - thers, liv - ing still In spite of dun - geon, fire and sword, O how our hearts beat high with joy When-e'er we hear that glo - rious word!

2. Faith of our fa - thers, we will strive To win all na - tions un - to Thee; And through the truth that comes from God Man - kind shall then in - deed be free. Faith of our fa - thers,

3. Faith of our fa - thers, we will love Both friend and foe in all our strife, And preach Thee, too, as love knows how By kind - ly words and vir - tuous life.

ho - ly faith, We will be true to Thee till death.

God's People

# Come, Holy Spirit, Come

71

Dorothy A. Thrupp

*Harmonischer Liederschatz*

1. Come, Ho - ly Spir - it, come; Oh, hear my hum - ble prayer!
2. Thy light, Thy love im - part, And let it ev - er be
3. Let Thy rich grace in - crease Through all my ear - ly days

Stoop down and make my heart Thy home, And shed Thy bless - ing there.
A ho - ly, hum - ble, hap - py, heart, A dwell - ing place for Thee.
The fruits of right - eous - ness and peace To Thine e - ter - nal praise.

# Gracious Spirit, Dove Divine

72

John Stocker

*Heilige Seelenlust*

1. Gracious Spir - it, Dove Di - vine, Let Thy light with - in me shine,
2. Let me nev - er from Thee stray, Keep me in the nar - row way,

All my guilt - y fears re - move, Fill me with Thy heav'n - ly love.
Fill my soul with joy di - vine, Keep me, Lord, for - ev - er Thine.

God's People—Pentecost

## 73         I Was Glad

Psalm 122:1

Mary Royer

I was glad when they said un - to me,

Let us go in - to the house of the Lord.

God's House

# Here in Our Father's House

Mrs. C. B. Palmer and Dorothy F. Poulton

Lowell Mason

1. Here in our Fa - ther's house We meet to sing and pray,
2. This is our Fa - ther's house We sing to Him to - day,

Our hearts are full of love and praise, We sing to Him to - day.
He hears each song of praise we sing, And lis-tens when we pray.

# We Love Our Church, O God

75

Stanza 1, Nan F. Heflin
Stanza 2, Clara Beers Blashfield

Aaron Williams

1. We love our church, O God We love to gath-er here
2. We love our church, O God This place of friendly cheer;

To wor-ship, work, and learn of Thee, With Chris-tian friends so dear.
We come to sing, to work, to pray To God who is ev - er near.

God's House

**76**  **When to Church I Go**

Caroline Kellogg

Dorothy West

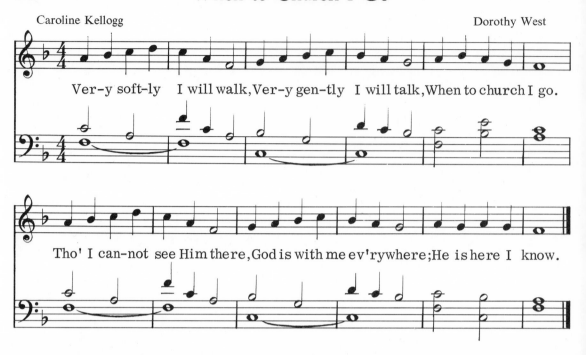

Ver-y soft-ly I will walk, Ver-y gen-tly I will talk, When to church I go.

Tho' I can-not see Him there, God is with me ev'rywhere; He is here I know.

**77**  **In Our Church We Gladly Sing**

Elizabeth Cringen Gardner, alt.

French Melody

In our church we glad - ly sing, And we al-so soft-ly pray,

Thank-ing God for ev - 'ry-thing, God, who loves us ev-'ry day.

God's House

# Holy Bible, Book Divine

John Barton
Stanza 2, alt.

Orlando Gibbons
Arr. by Paul G. Bunjes

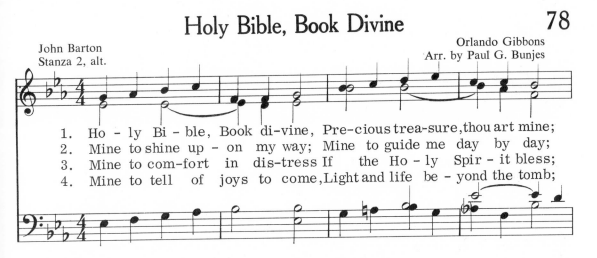

1. Ho - ly Bi - ble, Book di - vine, Pre-cious trea-sure, thou art mine;
2. Mine to shine up - on my way; Mine to guide me day by day;
3. Mine to com-fort in dis-tress If the Ho - ly Spir - it bless;
4. Mine to tell of joys to come, Light and life be - yond the tomb;

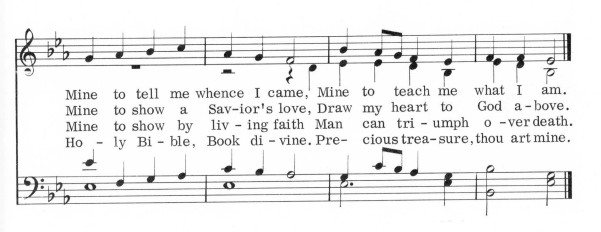

Mine to tell me whence I came, Mine to teach me what I am.
Mine to show a Sav-ior's love, Draw my heart to God a-bove.
Mine to show by liv - ing faith Man can tri - umph o - ver death.
Ho - ly Bi - ble, Book di - vine. Pre-cious trea-sure, thou art mine.

# Thou Wilt Keep Him in Perfect Peace

Isaiah 26:3

Charles Hutcheson
Har. by Derek Ferris

Thou wilt keep him in per-fect peace, Whose mind is stayed on Thee.

God's Word

# God Did So Love the World

John 3:16

Carey Bonner, alt.

God did so love the world He gave His on - ly Son the lost to save, That all who would in Him be - lieve Should ev - er - last - ing life re - ceive.

# The Bible Helps Me

Mabel Niedermeyer

Adapted from *Day's Psalter*

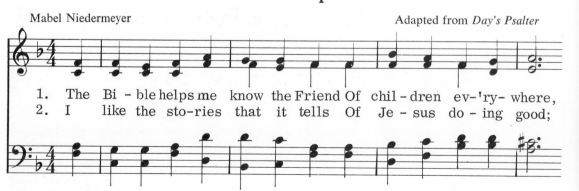

1. The Bi - ble helps me know the Friend Of chil - dren ev - 'ry - where,
2. I like the sto - ries that it tells Of Je - sus do - ing good;

God's Word

Who came to help us un-der-stand Our Fa-ther's love and care.
They help me act in friend-ly ways To do the things I should.

## To God's Most Holy House 82

Edith Lovell Thomas

*Pseaumes Octanie Geneva*
Arr. by Healey Willan

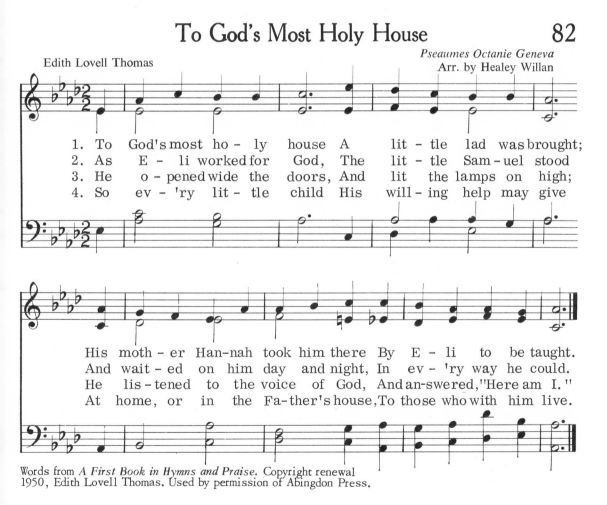

1. To God's most ho - ly house A lit - tle lad was brought;
2. As E - li worked for God, The lit - tle Sam - uel stood
3. He o - pened wide the doors, And lit the lamps on high;
4. So ev - 'ry lit - tle child His will - ing help may give

His moth - er Han-nah took him there By E - li to be taught.
And wait - ed on him day and night, In ev - 'ry way he could.
He lis - tened to the voice of God, And an-swered, "Here am I."
At home, or in the Fa-ther's house, To those who with him live.

God's Word

# For Stories Fine and True

Ethel L. Smither

Melchior Teschner

1. We thank Thee, O our Fa - ther, For sto - ries fine and true
2. We thank Thee, O our Fa - ther, For sto - ries fine and true

Of peo - ple in the Bi - ble Who knew and loved Thee too.
Of one who tried so glad - ly His Fa - ther's work to do.

They learned to serve Thee brave - ly, To help 'gainst pain and wrong;
We like to hear of Je - sus, So brave, so strong in need;

They won-dered at Thy good - ness; They praised in joy - ous song.
We thank Thee for the Bi - ble: His sto - ry there we read.

God's Word

## Thy Word Is Hid

84

Psalm 119

Harold Thiessen

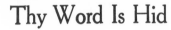

1. Thy Word is hid with-in my heart, That I sin not 'gainst Thee.
2. Bless-ed art Thou, O Lord my God, Teach Thy commandments true.
3. Thy pre-cepts will I med-i-tate, Re-spect un-to Thy ways.
4. Thy Word is to my feet a lamp, My path-ways light af-ford.

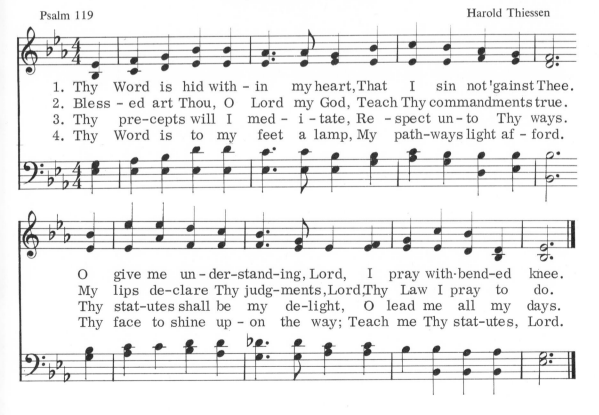

O give me un-der-stand-ing, Lord, I pray with-bend-ed knee.
My lips de-clare Thy judg-ments, Lord, Thy Law I pray to do.
Thy stat-utes shall be my de-light, O lead me all my days.
Thy face to shine up-on the way; Teach me Thy stat-utes, Lord.

God's Word

# The Best Book of All

Mary Royer

Charles Burkhart

The best book of all is the Bi - ble, It

tells a - bout Je - sus, God's Son, It

tells of the good home in heav - en, It

tells that God loves ev - 'ry one.

God's Word

# How Shall the Young Direct Their Way 86

Psalm 119:9-16
*The Psalter* 1912

Melody by Georg Josephi

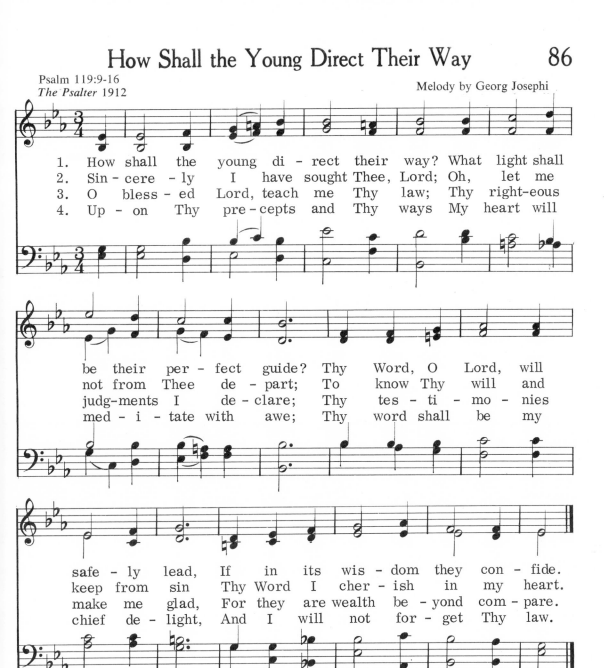

1. How shall the young di - rect their way? What light shall
2. Sin - cere - ly I have sought Thee, Lord; Oh, let me
3. O bless - ed Lord, teach me Thy law; Thy right-eous
4. Up - on Thy pre - cepts and Thy ways My heart will

be their per - fect guide? Thy Word, O Lord, will
not from Thee de - part; To know Thy will and
judg-ments I de - clare; Thy tes - ti - mo - nies
med - i - tate with awe; Thy word shall be my

safe - ly lead, If in its wis - dom they con - fide.
keep from sin Thy Word I cher - ish in my heart.
make me glad, For they are wealth be - yond com - pare.
chief de - light, And I will not for - get Thy law.

# The Golden Rule 87

Ruth Carper Eitzen

Ruth Carper Eitzen

What - e - ver you wish that men would do to you, do so to them.

God's Word

**88**      **In Christ There Is No East or West**

John Oxenham                                 Alexander R. Reinagle

1. In Christ there is no East or West, In Him no South or North;
2. In Him shall true hearts ev-'ry-where Their high communion find;
3. Join hands, then, brothers of the faith, What-e'er your race may be.
4. In Christ now meet both East and West, In Him meet South and North;

But one great fel-low-ship of love Through-out the whole wide earth.
His ser-vice is the gold-en cord Close bind-ing all mankind.
Who serves my Fa-ther as a son Is sure-ly kin to me.
All Christ-ly souls are one in Him Through-out the whole wide earth.

**89**      **We Pray for Children O'er the Sea**

Florence O'Keane Whelan                              Old Tune
                                       Arr. by Florence O'Keane Whelan

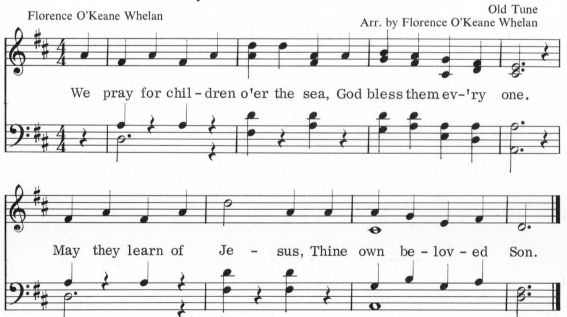

We pray for chil-dren o'er the sea, God bless them ev-'ry one.

May they learn of Je-sus, Thine own be-lov-ed Son.

The Church Around the World

# The Many, Many Children

Wilhelmina D'A Stephens

Lowell Mason

1. The man-y, man-y chil-dren Throughout the world so fair
2. Then let us, all His chil-dren, At home, at work, at play

Are chil-dren of our Fa-ther, Who keeps them in His care.
Be quick to help each oth-er, Our Fa-ther's will o-bey,

No mat-ter what their col-or, He loves them one and all;
That all the wide world's chil-dren In hap-pi-ness may live,

No mat-ter where they're liv-ing, He hears them when they call.
What-e'er their race or col-or, And praise to Him may give.

The Church Around the World

**91**  **Let the Savior's Gentle Call**

Author Unknown

Scheffler's *Heilige Seelenlust*

1. Let the Sav-ior's gen-tle call Reach the heart of one and all,
2. Far and nigh the good news bring:"Je-sus Christ is Lord and King!"
3. Print the Word till all may read: "Je- sus is the Friend in need."

That the whole round world may own Christ is King, and Christ a-lone.
Flash the word that God is near O'er the air till all may hear.
Preach the word on ev-'ry shore Till all men do God a - dore.

**92**  **I Give Thee Thanks with All My Heart**

Miriam Drury

Carl F. Mueller

I give Thee thanks with all my heart For those who do their loving part To

make our world a hap - py place For ev-'ry child of ev - 'ry race.

The Church Around the World

# O Grant Us Lord, Thy Peace

Imogene Humphrey

*St. Alban's Tune Book*
Arr. by James W. Bixel

1. O grant us Lord, Thy peace, Let wars for - ev - er cease,
2. Let na - tions leave the sword And take God's Ho - ly Word,

Let na - tions dwell in peace and love As in Thy home a - bove.
Drive out all sel - fish-ness and greed Then peace shall reign in-deed.

The Church Around the World

**94**  **O God of Love, O King of Peace**

Henry Baker                                    Henry Baker

1. O God of love, O King of peace, Make wars through-
2. Re - mem - ber, Lord, Thy works of old, The won - ders
3. Whom shall we trust but Thee, O Lord? Where rest but
4. Where saints and an - gels dwell a - bove, All hearts are

out the world to cease; The wrath of sin - ful
that our fa - thers told; Re - mem - ber not our
on Thy faith - ful word? None ev - er called on
knit in ho - ly love; O bind us in that

man re - strain; Give peace, O God, give peace a - gain!
sin's dark stain; Give peace, O God, give peace a - gain!
Thee in vain; Give peace, O God, give peace a - gain!
heav'n - ly chain; Give peace, O God, give peace a - gain!

The Church Around the World

# Remember All God's Children

95

Percy Dearmer

Melody from *Gesangbuch mit Noten,* arr.

1. Re - mem - ber all God's chil - dren, Who yet have nev - er heard The truth that comes from Je - sus, The glo - ry of His word, The truth that comes from Je - sus, The glo - ry of His word.

2. God bless the men and wo - men Who serve Him o - ver - sea; God raise up more to help them To set the na - tions free, God raise up more to help them To set the na - tions free.

3. Till all the dis - tant peo - ple In ev - 'ry for - eign place Shall un - der - stand His king - dom And come in - to His grace Shall un - der - stand His king - dom And come in - to His grace.

The Church Around the World

## 96    Jesus, Friend of Little Children

Walter John Mathams

Martin Shaw

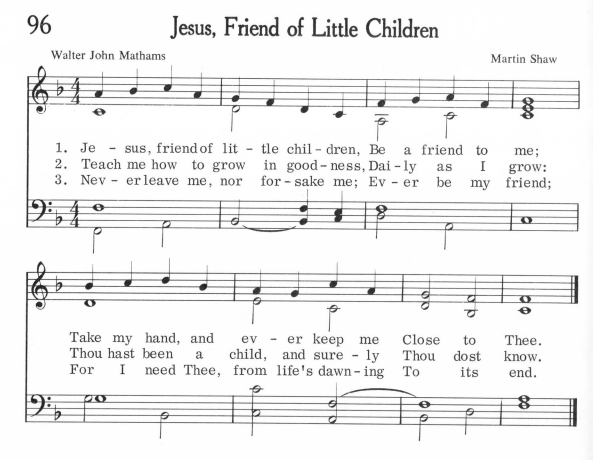

1. Je - sus, friend of lit - tle chil - dren, Be a friend to me;
2. Teach me how to grow in good - ness, Dai - ly as I grow:
3. Nev - er leave me, nor for - sake me; Ev - er be my friend;

Take my hand, and ev - er keep me Close to Thee.
Thou hast been a child, and sure - ly Thou dost know.
For I need Thee, from life's dawn - ing To its end.

Jesus, Our Friend

# Jesus Loves Me

Anna Bartlett Warner                                    William B. Bradbury, slightly alt.

1. Je - sus loves me! this I know, For the Bi - ble tells me so;
2. Je - sus loves me! He who died, Heav-en's gate, to o - pen wide;
3. Je - sus loves me! loves me still, Tho' I'm ver - y weak and ill;
4. Je - sus loves me! He will stay Close be - side me all the way;

Lit - tle ones to Him be - long, They are weak, but He is strong.
He will wash a - way my sin, Let His lit - tle child come in.
From His shin - ing throne on high, Comes to watch me where I lie.
If I love Him, when I die He will take me home on high.

Yes, Je - sus loves me, Yes, Je - sus loves me,

Yes, Je - sus loves me, The Bi - ble tells me so.

## Jesus liebt mich ganz gewiss

1 Jesus liebt mich ganz gewiss,
  denn die Bibel sagt mir dies.
  Alle Kinder schwach und klein,
  lad't er herzlich zu sich ein.

2 Jesus liebt mich, denn sein Blut
  floss am Kreuz auch mir zu gut.
  Er macht mich von Sünden rein,
  wenn ich zu ihm kehre ein.

3 Jesus liebt mich, er mein Hirt,
  führt mich recht, wenn ich verirrt.
  Bleib' ich hier auf Erden sein,
  führt er mich zum Himmel ein.

Refrain;
Ja, Jesus liebt mich,
ja, Jesus liebt mich,
ja, Jesus liebt mich,
die Bibel sagt mir dies.

Jesus, Our Friend

**98**

# Let Me Learn of Jesus

Fanny J. Crosby

J. F. Swift

1. Let me learn of Je - sus; He is kind to me;
2. When I go to Je - sus, He will hear me pray,
3. Let me think of Je - sus; He is full of love,
4. Oh, how good is Je - sus! May He hold my hand

Once He died to save me, Nailed up - on the tree.
Make me pure and ho - ly, Take my sins a - way.
Look - ing down up - on me From His throne a - bove.
And at last re - ceive me To a bet - ter land.

**99**

# Jesus Was a Loving Teacher

Wilhelmina D'A Stephens

Charlotte A. Barnard

1. Je - sus was a lov - ing teach - er, Help - ing peo - ple day by day
2. Je - sus was a pa - tient teach - er, Want - ing all to learn God's will.
3. God, we thank Thee for this teach - er, And our praise to Thee we give,

Know the love of God our Fa - ther, Teach - ing them to love and pray.
Tell - ing sto - ries they'd re - mem - ber Sto - ries that we're read - ing still.
For His love and for His pa - tience, Show - ing peo - ple how to live.

Jesus, Our Friend

# Jesus, Our Friend

Elizabeth McE. Shields

Elda Flett Baker
Arr. by J. Harold Moyer

1. When Je - sus was a ba - by boy He slept up - on the hay,
2. He helped His moth - er in the home, He played like you and me;
3. When Je - sus grew to be a man He made the sick ones well,
4. Dear Je - sus is the children's friend; He held them on His knee;

And then He grew and worked and played Each glad and hap - py day.
And ev - 'ry day He did o - bey; A hap - py boy was He.
And made folk good and lov - ing by The sto - ries that He'd tell.
He took them in His arms and said, "Let chil - dren come to me."

# Something Kind

Sallie Futrell Stone

Sallie Futrell Stone
Arr. by George Wiebe

Je - sus healed the sick, Je - sus helped the blind;

Ev - 'ry day He went a - bout Do - ing some-thing kind.

**102**

# Jesus, Lead Me Day by Day

Author Unknown

George C. Strattner

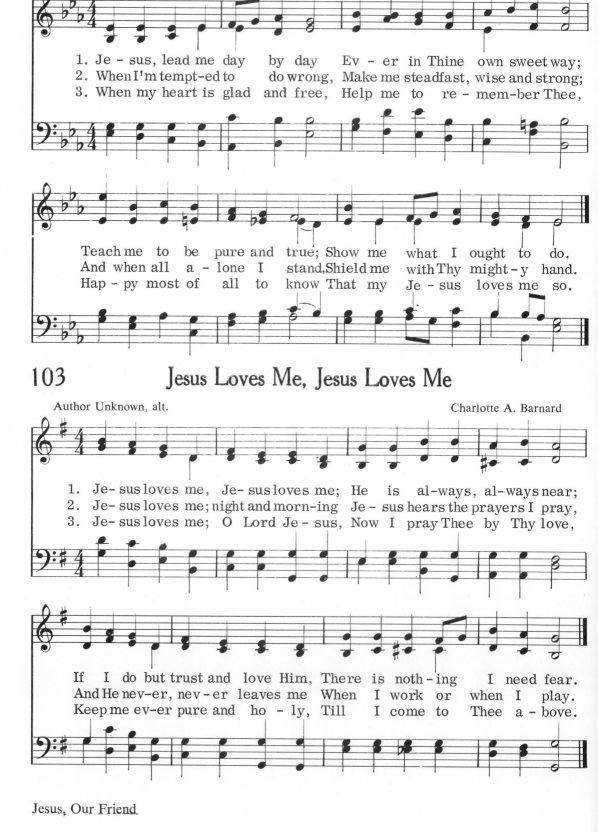

1. Je - sus, lead me day   by day   Ev - er in Thine   own sweet way;
2. When I'm tempt-ed to   do wrong, Make me steadfast, wise and strong;
3. When my heart is glad   and free, Help me to   re - mem-ber Thee,

Teach me to be pure and true; Show me   what I ought to do.
And when all a - lone I stand, Shield me   with Thy might-y hand.
Hap - py most of all to know That my   Je - sus loves me so.

**103**

# Jesus Loves Me, Jesus Loves Me

Author Unknown, alt.

Charlotte A. Barnard

1. Je - sus loves me, Je - sus loves me; He   is al-ways, al-ways near;
2. Je - sus loves me; night and morn-ing Je - sus hears the prayers I pray,
3. Je - sus loves me; O Lord Je - sus, Now I pray Thee by Thy love,

If   I do but trust and love Him, There is noth - ing   I need fear.
And He nev-er, nev-er leaves me When   I work or   when I play.
Keep me ev-er pure and ho - ly, Till   I come to   Thee a - bove.

Jesus, Our Friend

# The Children's Friend

**104**

Jessie Eleanor Moore

Helen H. Lemmel

1. Long a-go the lit-tle chil-dren Gath-ered close at Je-sus' knee,
2. Come and lis-ten to the sto-ry, Friend of chil-dren still is He,

For His kind-ly smile said gen-tly, "I love them and they love me."
Lis-ten then and whis-per soft-ly, "I love Him and He loves me."

# My Best Friend Is Jesus

**105**

Mildred Adair Stagg

Mildred Adair Stagg

1. My best friend is Je-sus, Love Him! Love Him!
2. My best friend is Je-sus, Thank Him! Thank Him!
3. My best friend is Je-sus, *

My best friend is Je-sus, Love Him!
My best friend is Je-sus, Thank Him!
My best friend is Je-sus, *

*The children may suggest other stanzas.

Jesus, Our Friend

# 106  Lord, I Want to Be a Christian

Traditional

Arr. by J. Harold Moyer

1. Lord, I want to be a Chris-tian In-a my heart, in-a my heart, Lord, I want to be a Chris-tian In-a my heart.
2. Lord, I want to be more lov-ing In-a my heart, in-a my heart, Lord, I want to be more lov-ing In-a my heart.
3. Lord, I want to be more ho-ly In-a my heart, in-a my heart, Lord, I want to be more ho-ly In-a my heart.
4. Lord, I want to be like Je-sus In-a my heart, in-a my heart, Lord, I want to be like Je-sus In-a my heart.

In-a my heart, In-a my heart, In-a my heart, In-a my heart,

Lord, I want to be a Chris-tian In-a my heart.
Lord, I want to be more lov-ing In-a my heart.
Lord, I want to be more ho-ly In-a my heart.
Lord, I want to be like Je-sus In-a my heart.

Serving Jesus

# My Body Is God's Temple

Elizabeth A. Showalter

George F. Root

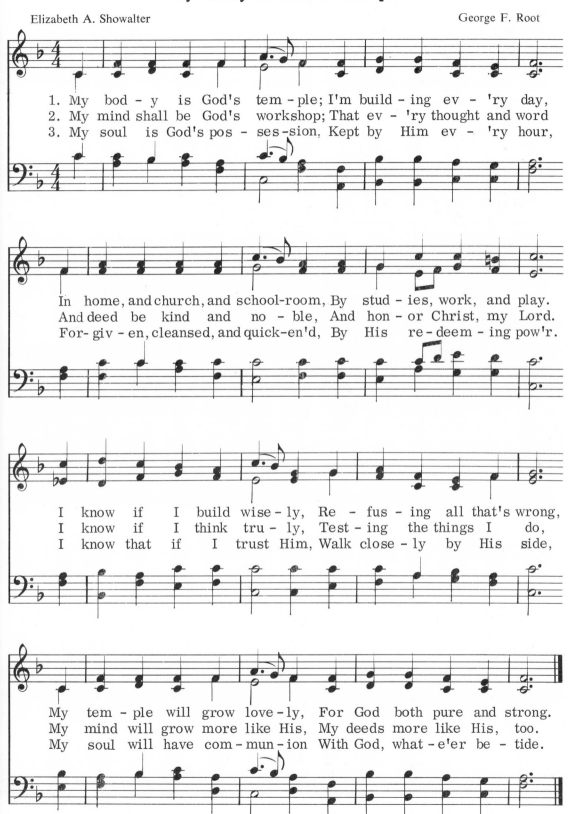

1. My bod-y is God's tem-ple; I'm build-ing ev-'ry day,
2. My mind shall be God's workshop; That ev-'ry thought and word
3. My soul is God's pos-ses-sion, Kept by Him ev-'ry hour,

In home, and church, and school-room, By stud-ies, work, and play.
And deed be kind and no-ble, And hon-or Christ, my Lord.
For-giv-en, cleansed, and quick-en'd, By His re-deem-ing pow'r.

I know if I build wise-ly, Re-fus-ing all that's wrong,
I know if I think tru-ly, Test-ing the things I do,
I know that if I trust Him, Walk close-ly by His side,

My tem-ple will grow love-ly, For God both pure and strong.
My mind will grow more like His, My deeds more like His, too.
My soul will have com-mun-ion With God, what-e'er be-tide.

Serving Jesus

# 108    I Think When I Read That Sweet Story of Old

Jemima Luke

Greek Folk Song
Arr. by William B. Bradbury

1. I think when I read that sweet sto - ry of old, When
2. I wish that His hands had been placed on my head, That His

Je - sus was here a - mong men, How He called lit - tle chil - dren as
arm had been thrown a - round me, And that I might have seen His kind

lambs to His fold, I should like to have been with them then.
look when He said, "Let the lit - tle ones come un - to me."

# 109                          Following Christ

Josephine L. Baldwin

English Traditional Melody, coll. and arr. by
Lucy Broadwood, har. by R. Vaughan Williams

1. Sav - ior, in the words I say May I fol - low Thine own way;
2. Show me how to play each game Fair and square, as in Thy Name;
3. In my home, at play, at school, May I keep the Gold - en Rule;

Serving Jesus

And in all the deeds I do Show a spir-it fair and true.
Lose the con-test if I must, But in ev-'ry act be just.
Brave-ly face the hard-est test, Love my neigh-bors, do my best.

## Jacob's Ladder 110

Traditional                                                     Traditional

1. We are climb-ing Ja-cob's lad-der, We are climb-ing Ja-cob's lad-der, We are climb-ing Ja-cob's lad-der Sol-diers of the cross.

2  Ev'ry round goes higher, higher,
3  Sinner, do you love your Jesus?
4  If you love Him, why not serve Him?
5  We are climbing higher, higher.

Serving Jesus

# I Sing a Song of the Saints of God

Lesbia Scott

John H. Hopkins

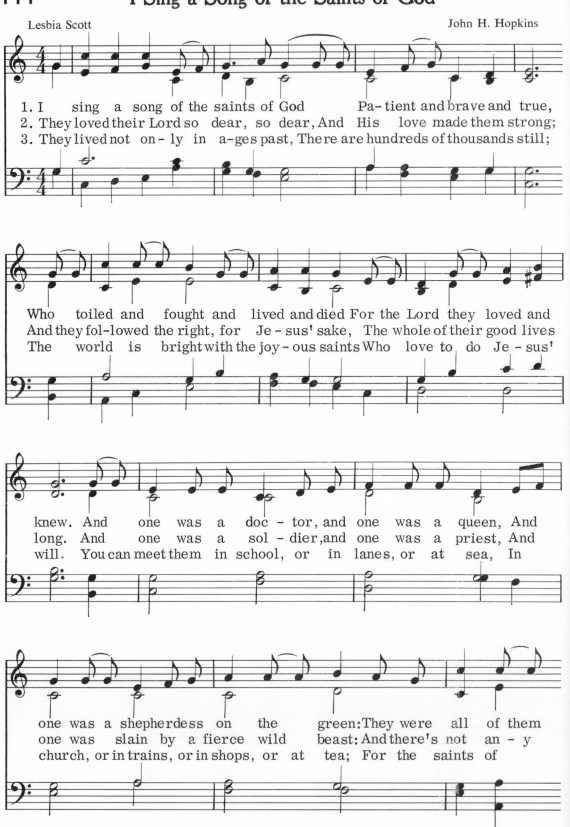

1. I sing a song of the saints of God Pa-tient and brave and true,
2. They loved their Lord so dear, so dear, And His love made them strong;
3. They lived not on-ly in a-ges past, There are hundreds of thousands still;

Who toiled and fought and lived and died For the Lord they loved and
And they fol-lowed the right, for Je-sus' sake, The whole of their good lives
The world is bright with the joy-ous saints Who love to do Je-sus'

knew. And one was a doc-tor, and one was a queen, And
long. And one was a sol-dier, and one was a priest, And
will. You can meet them in school, or in lanes, or at sea, In

one was a shepherdess on the green: They were all of them
one was slain by a fierce wild beast: And there's not an-y
church, or in trains, or in shops, or at tea; For the saints of

Serving Jesus

saints of God, and I mean, God help-ing, to be one too.
rea - son, no, not the least, Why I should-n't be one too.
God are just folk like me, And I mean to be one too.

## I Would Follow Jesus

112

Frank von Christierson

German Folk Song
Arr. by Roberta Bitgood

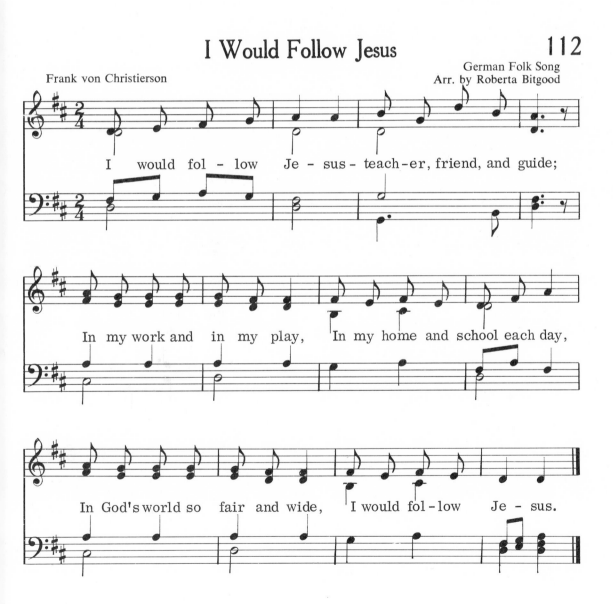

I would fol - low Je - sus - teach-er, friend, and guide;

In my work and in my play, In my home and school each day,

In God's world so fair and wide, I would fol-low Je - sus.

Serving Jesus

**113**

# A Prayer to Jesus

Frances Weld Danielson

Henry Baker

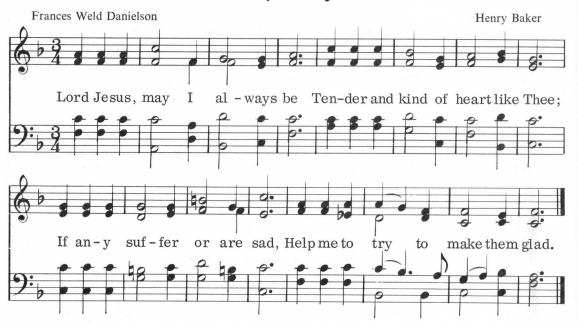

Lord Jesus, may I al-ways be Ten-der and kind of heart like Thee;

If an-y suf-fer or are sad, Help me to try to make them glad.

**114**

# God My Father, Loving Me

George Wallace Briggs

Melody from Justin Heinrich Knecht

1. God my Fa-ther lov-ing me, Gave His Son my friend to be:
2. Je-sus still re-mains the same As in days of old He came;
3. How can I re-pay Thy love, Lord of all the hosts a-bove?
4. I have but my-self to give, Let me for Thy ser-vice live;

Gave His Son my form to take, And to suf-fer for my sake.
As my broth-er by my side, Still He seeks my steps to guide.
What have I, a child, to bring Un-to Thee, Thou heav'n-ly King?
Let me fol-low, day by day, Where Thou show-est me the way.

Serving Jesus

# Savior, While My Heart Is Tender 115

John Burton, the younger                                    Old French Melody

1. Sav-ior, while my heart is ten-der, I would yield that heart to Thee;
2. Take me now, Lord Je-sus, take me; Let my youth-ful heart be Thine;
3. Send me, Lord, where Thou wilt send me, On-ly do Thou guide my way;

All my pow'rs to Thee surrender, Thine and on-ly Thine to be.
Thy de-vot-ed servant make me; Fill my soul with love di-vine.
May Thy grace through life at-tend me, Glad-ly then shall I o-bey.

4 May this solemn consecration
Never once forgotten be;
Let it know no revocation,
Registered, confirmed by Thee.

5 Thine I am, O Lord, forever,
To Thy service set apart;
Suffer me to leave Thee never;
Seal Thine image on my heart.

Serving Jesus

**116**

# Fairest Lord Jesus

German, 14th century

Silesian Folk Song
Arr. by R. S. Willis

1. Fair-est Lord Je - sus, Rul - er of all na - ture, O Thou of
2. Fair are the mead - ows, Fair - er still the wood-lands, Robed in the
3. Fair is the sun - shine, Fair - er still the moon-light, And all the

God and man the Son; Thee will I cher - ish,
bloom - ing garb of spring; Je - sus is fair - er,
twink - ling, star - ry host; Je - sus shines bright - er,

Thee will I hon - or, Thou, my soul's glo-ry, joy and crown.
Je - sus is pur - er, Who makes the woe-ful heart to sing.
Je - sus shines pur - er Than all the an-gels heaven can boast.

## Schönster Herr Jesu

1. Schönster Herr Jesu,
   Herrscher aller Enden,
   Gottes and Mariae Sohn!
   Dich will ich lieben,
   dich will ich ehren,
   du meiner Seelen Freud und Kron!

2. Schön sind die Wälder,
   schöner sind die Felder
   in der schönen Frühlingszeit.
   Jesus ist schöner,
   Jesus ist reiner,
   der unser traurig Herz erfreut.

3. Schön leucht't der Monde,
   schöner leucht't die Sonne,
   schön die Sternlein allzumal.
   Jesus leucht't schöner,
   Jesus leucht't reiner,
   als all die Engel im Himmelssaal.

Serving Jesus

# In Our Work and in Our Play

Whitfield G. Wills

English Melody

1. In our work and in our play, Je - sus, ev - er
2. May we in Thy strength sub - due E - vil tem - pers,
3. Chil - dren of the King are we! May we loy - al

with us stay; May we al - ways strive to be
words un - true, Thoughts im - pure, and deeds un - kind,
to Him be; Try to please Him ev - 'ry day,

True and faith - ful un - to Thee. Then we truth - ful -
All things hate - ful to Thy mind. Then we truth - ful -
In our work and in our play. Then we truth - ful -

ly can sing, We are chil - dren of the King.
ly can sing, We are chil - dren of the King.
ly can sing, We are chil - dren of the King.

Serving Jesus

## 118     Dear Lord, We Give Our Youth to Thee

Calvin W. Laufer

Albert L. Peace

1. Dear Lord, we give our youth to Thee, In an-swer to Thy call,
2. Show us each day what we can do, Where'er our paths may lead,
3. May friend - ly acts, fair play, and love Bring cheer to all a-round,
4. We've heard Thy call, and take our stand, We know not what's be-fore;

And pray our hearts may loy-al be To love Thee best of all.
To dare the right, to seek the true, To com-fort those in need.
That this fair earth, like heav'n a--bove, May with Thy peace a-bound.
But we are Thine with heart and hand, To serve Thee ev - er-more.

## 119     Little Things

Julia A. Carney

Composer Unknown

1. Lit - tle drops of wa - ter, Lit - tle grains of sand,
2. Lit - tle deeds of kind - ness, Lit - tle words of love,

Make the might-y o - cean, And the pleas - ant land.
Help to make earth hap - py, Like the heav-en a - bove.

Serving Jesus

# Two Little Hands

W. A. Ogden

W. A. Ogden
Arr. by James W. Bixel

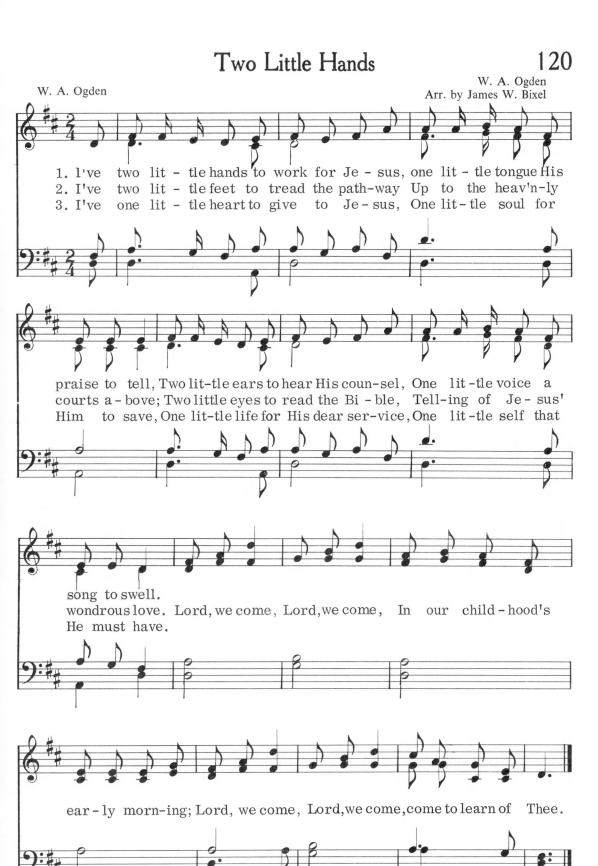

1. I've two lit-tle hands to work for Je-sus, one lit-tle tongue His
2. I've two lit-tle feet to tread the path-way Up to the heav'n-ly
3. I've one lit-tle heart to give to Je-sus, One lit-tle soul for

praise to tell, Two lit-tle ears to hear His coun-sel, One lit-tle voice a
courts a-bove; Two little eyes to read the Bi-ble, Tell-ing of Je-sus'
Him to save, One lit-tle life for His dear ser-vice, One lit-tle self that

song to swell.
wondrous love. Lord, we come, Lord, we come, In our child-hood's
He must have.

ear-ly morn-ing; Lord, we come, Lord, we come, come to learn of Thee.

Serving Jesus

# Tell Me the Stories of Jesus

W. H. Parker

F. A. Challinor

1. Tell me the sto - ries of Je - sus I love to hear;
2. First let me hear how the chil - dren Stood round His knee;
3. In - to the cit - y I'd fol - low The chil - dren's band,
4. Tell me, in ac - cents of won - der, How rolled the sea,

Things I would ask Him to tell me If He were here;
And I shall fan - cy His bless - ing Rest - ing on me:
Wav - ing a branch of the palm - tree High in my hand;
Toss - ing the boat in a tem - pest On Gal - i - lee!

Scenes by the way - side, Tales of the sea,
Words full of kind - ness, Deeds full of grace,
One of His her - alds, Yes, I would sing
And how the Mas - ter, Read - y and kind,

Sto - ries of Je - sus, Tell them to me.
All in the love - light Of Je - sus' face.
Loud - est ho - san - nas! Je - sus is King!
Chid - ed the bil - lows, And hushed the wind.

Serving Jesus

# O Jesus, Once a Nazareth Boy

Stanza 1, Harry M. Hedge
Stanza 2, Ethel W. Trout

Henry S. Cutler

1. O Je-sus, once a Naza-reth boy, And tempt-ed like as we,
   All in-ward foes help us de-stroy, And spot-less all to be.
   We trust Thee for the grace to win the high vic-to-rious goal,
   Where pur-i-ty shall con-quer sin In Christ-like self-con-trol.

2. O Je-sus, once a Naza-reth boy, Who toiled through happy days,
   May we our dai-ly tasks en-joy, And work with songs of praise.
   At school, at home we fol-low Thee, with all our heart and soul,
   Work hard, play fair, and try to be Like Thee in self-con-trol.

Serving Jesus

## 123 Take My Life and Let It Be

Frances R. Havergal

Henri A. C. Malan

1. Take my life and let it be Con-se-crat-ed,
2. Take my hands, and let them move At the im-pulse
3. Take my voice, and let me sing, Al-ways, on-ly,
4. Take my will and make it Thine, It shall be no

Lord, to Thee; Take my mo-ments and my days; Let them flow in
of Thy love. Take my feet, and let them be Swift and beau-ti-
for my King. Take my lips, and let them be Filled with mes-sa-
long-er mine: Take my heart, it is Thine own, It shall be Thy

cease-less praise. Let them flow in cease-less praise.
ful for Thee. Swift and beau-ti - ful for Thee.
ges from Thee. Filled with mes - sa - ges from Thee.
roy - al throne. It shall be Thy roy - al throne.

Serving Jesus

## Come with Hearts Rejoicing

Lina A. Rauschenberg

Arr. from Op. 61, by Ludwig van Beethoven
Lina A. Rauschenberg, alt.

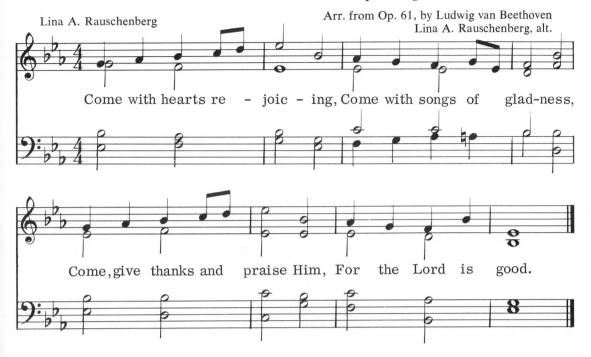

Come with hearts re - joic - ing, Come with songs of glad-ness,

Come, give thanks and praise Him, For the Lord is good.

## All People That on Earth Do Dwell

Psalm 100
Ascribed to William Kethe, *Scottish Psalter*

Melody from *Genevan Psalter*
Arr. by Louis Bourgeois

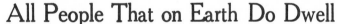

1. All peo - ple that on earth do dwell, Sing to the Lord with cheerful voice.
2. Know that the Lord is God in - deed; With-out our aid He did us make;
3. O en - ter then His gates with praise, Approach with joy His courts unto;
4. For why? the Lord our God is good; His mer - cy is for ev - er sure;

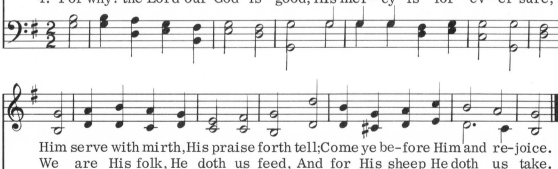

Him serve with mirth, His praise forth tell; Come ye be-fore Him and re - joice.
We are His folk, He doth us feed, And for His sheep He doth us take.
Praise, laud, and bless His name always, For it is seem-ly so to do.
His truth at all times firm-ly stood, And shall from age to age en-dure.

Praise

## 126     A Gladsome Hymn of Praise

Ambrose N. Blatchford

Composer Unknown
Arr. by J. Harold Moyer

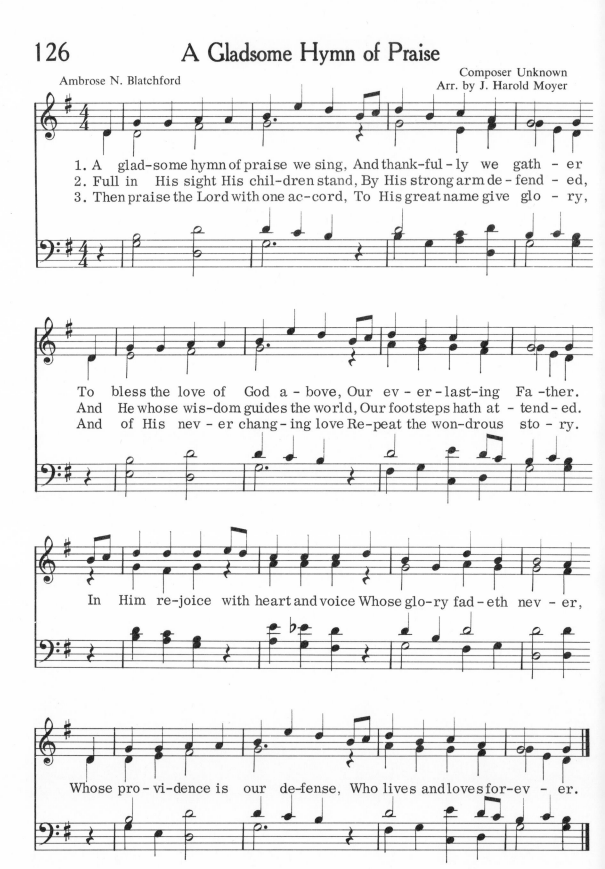

1. A glad-some hymn of praise we sing, And thank-ful - ly we gath - er
2. Full in His sight His chil-dren stand, By His strong arm de - fend - ed,
3. Then praise the Lord with one ac-cord, To His great name give glo - ry,

To bless the love of God a - bove, Our ev - er - last-ing Fa - ther.
And He whose wis-dom guides the world, Our footsteps hath at - tend - ed,
And of His nev - er chang - ing love Re - peat the won-drous sto - ry.

In Him re-joice with heart and voice Whose glo - ry fad - eth nev - er,

Whose pro - vi-dence is our de-fense, Who lives and loves for-ev - er.

Praise

# Holy, Holy, Holy

Reginald Heber

John B. Dykes

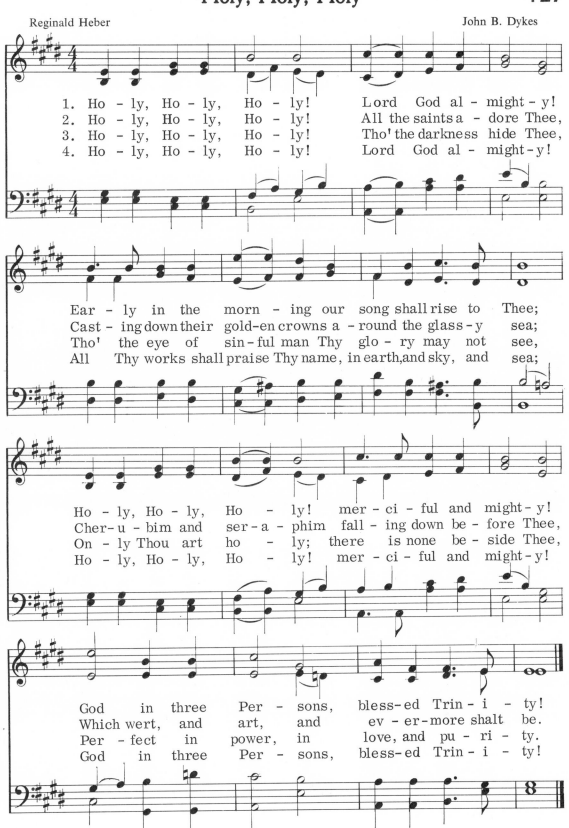

1. Ho - ly, Ho - ly, Ho - ly! Lord God al - might - y!
2. Ho - ly, Ho - ly, Ho - ly! All the saints a - dore Thee,
3. Ho - ly, Ho - ly, Ho - ly! Tho' the darkness hide Thee,
4. Ho - ly, Ho - ly, Ho - ly! Lord God al - might - y!

Ear - ly in the morn - ing our song shall rise to Thee;
Cast - ing down their gold-en crowns a - round the glass-y sea;
Tho' the eye of sin-ful man Thy glo - ry may not see,
All Thy works shall praise Thy name, in earth, and sky, and sea;

Ho - ly, Ho - ly, Ho - ly! mer - ci - ful and might - y!
Cher - u - bim and ser - a - phim fall - ing down be - fore Thee,
On - ly Thou art ho - ly; there is none be - side Thee,
Ho - ly, Ho - ly, Ho - ly! mer - ci - ful and might - y!

God in three Per - sons, bless-ed Trin - i - ty!
Which wert, and art, and ev - er-more shalt be.
Per - fect in power, in love, and pu - ri - ty.
God in three Per - sons, bless-ed Trin - i - ty!

Praise

# Children of Jerusalem Sang the Praise

John Henley

Curwen's *Tune Book*
Arr. by J. Harold Moyer

1. Chil - dren of Je - ru - sa - lem Sang the praise of
2. We are taught to love the Lord, We are taught to
3. Par - ents, teach - ers, old, and young, All u - nite to

Je - sus' name: Chil - dren, too, of mod - ern days Join to
read His Word; We are taught the way to heaven: Praise for
swell the song; High - er and yet high - er rise, Till ho -

sing the Sav - ior's praise.
all to God be given. Hark, hark, hark! while infant voi - ces sing,
san - nas fill the skies.

Hark, hark, hark! while in - fant voic - es sing Loud ho - san - nas,

Praise

Loud ho - san - nas, Loud ho - san - nas to our King.

## Come Ye Children, Praise the Savior 129

*Bible Class Magazine*, alt.

Johann B. Koenig
Arr. by Paul G. Bunjes

1. Come ye chil - dren, praise the Savior; He re - gards you from a - bove.
2. When the anx - ious moth - ers round Him With their tender infants pressed,
3. Up in yon - der hap - py re - gions An - gels sound the cho - rus high;

Praise Him for His great sal - va - tion; Praise Him for His pre - cious love.
He with o - pen arms re - ceived them, And the lit - tle ones He blessed.
Twice ten thou - sand times ten thousand Send His prais - es through the sky.

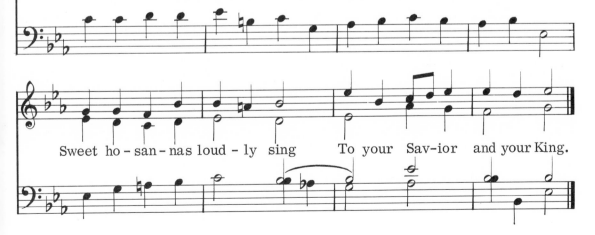

Sweet ho - san - nas loud - ly sing To your Sav - ior and your King.

# 130 Now Thank We All Our God

Martin Rinkart
Tr. by Catherine Winkworth

Johann Crüger

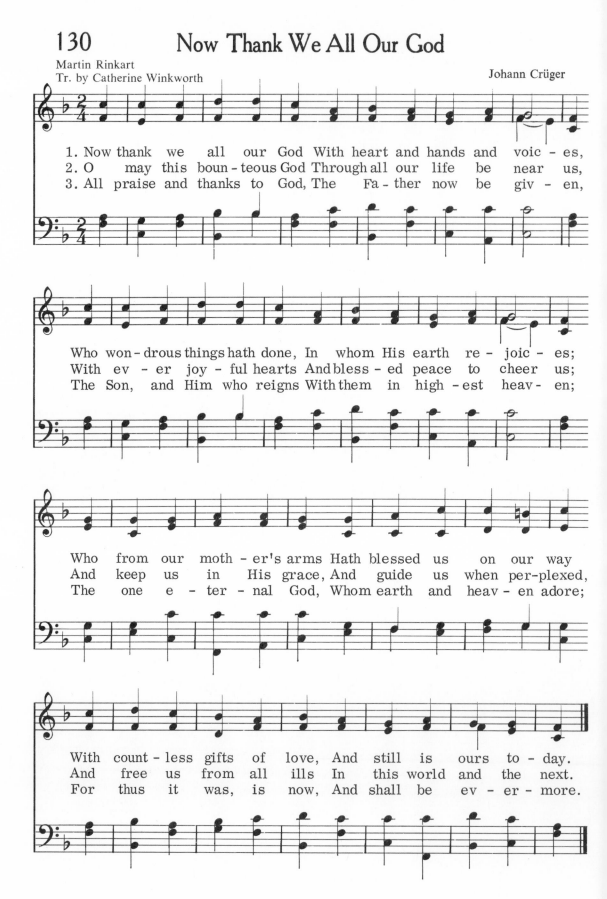

1. Now thank we all our God With heart and hands and voic - es,
2. O may this boun - teous God Through all our life be near us,
3. All praise and thanks to God, The Fa - ther now be giv - en,

Who won - drous things hath done, In whom His earth re - joic - es;
With ev - er joy - ful hearts And bless - ed peace to cheer us;
The Son, and Him who reigns With them in high - est heav - en;

Who from our moth - er's arms Hath blessed us on our way
And keep us in His grace, And guide us when per-plexed,
The one e - ter - nal God, Whom earth and heav - en adore;

With count - less gifts of love, And still is ours to - day.
And free us from all ills In this world and the next.
For thus it was, is now, And shall be ev - er - more.

Praise

# Nun danket alle Gott

1 Nun danket alle Gott
mit Herzen, Mund und Händen,
der grosse Dinge tut
an uns und allen Enden;
der uns von Mutterleib
und Kindesbeinen an
unzählig viel zu gut
bis hieher hat getan.

2 Der ewig reiche Gott
woll uns bei unserm Leben
ein immer fröhlich Herz
und edlen Frieden geben,
und uns in seiner Gnad
erhalten fort und fort,
und uns aus aller Not
erlösen hier und dort.

3 Lob, Ehr und Preis sei Gott,
dem Vater und dem Sohne
und dem, der beiden gleich
im höchsten Himmelsthrone,
dem dreieinigen Gott;
als der anfänglich war
und ist und bleiben wird
jetzund und immerdar.

# When the Master Calls Me Home 131

Author Unknown

From *Songs Along the Mahantonga*
Arr. by James W. Bixel

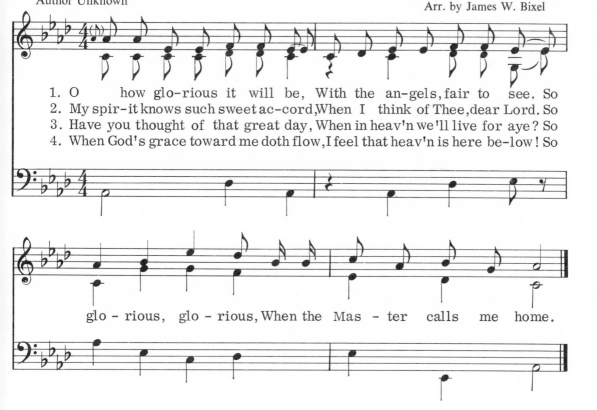

1. O     how glo-rious it will be, With the an-gels, fair to    see. So
2. My spir-it knows such sweet ac-cord, When I  think of Thee, dear Lord. So
3. Have you thought of  that great day, When in heav'n we'll live for aye? So
4. When God's grace toward me doth flow, I feel that heav'n is here be-low! So

glo - rious,  glo - rious, When the Mas - ter   calls   me   home.

## 132     Joyful, Joyful, We Adore Thee

Henry van Dyke

Arr. from Beethoven

1. Joy - ful, joy - ful, we a - dore Thee, God of glo - ry, Lord of love;
2. All Thy works with joy surround Thee, Earth and heaven reflect Thy rays,
3. Thou art giv - ing and for - giv - ing, Ev - er blessing, ev - er blest,
4. Mor - tals, join the might - y cho - rus Which the morning stars be - gan;

Hearts un-fold like flowers before Thee, Prais-ing Thee their sun a - bove.
Stars and an-gels sing a-round Thee, Cen - ter of un - broken praise.
Well-spring of the joy of liv - ing, O - cean depth of hap - py rest!
Fa - ther love is reign-ing o'er us, Broth-er love binds man to man.

Melt the clouds of sin and sad-ness, Drive the dark of doubt a - way;
Field and for - est, vale and mountain, Blooming mead-ow, flashing sea,
Thou our Fa - ther, Christ our Broth-er, All who live in love are Thine;
Ev - er singing, march we on-ward, Vic - tors in the midst of strife,

Giv - er of im - mor-tal gladness, Fill us with the light of day.
Chant-ing bird and flow-ing foun-tain, Call us to re - joice in Thee.
Teach us how to love each oth - er, Lift us to the joy di - vine.
Joy - ful mu-sic lifts us sunward In the triumph song of life.

Praise

# Praise Him, Praise Him

133

Author Unknown

Composer Unknown
Arr. by Hubert P. Main

1. Praise Him, praise Him, all ye little chil-dren; God is love, God is love,
2. Love Him, love Him, all ye lit-tle chil-dren; God is love, God is love,
3. Thank Him, thank Him, all ye lit-tle chil-dren; God is love, God is love,
4. Help Him, help Him, all ye lit-tle chil-dren; God is love, God is love,

Praise Him, praise Him, all ye little children; God is love, God is love.
Love Him, love Him, all ye lit-tle children; God is love, God is love.
Thank Him, thank Him, all ye lit-tle children; God is love, God is love.
Help Him, help Him, all ye lit-tle children; God is love, God is love.

# Alleluia

134

Traditional

Al - le - lu - ia, Al - le - lu - ia

A - — men A - — men.

## 135 We Thank Thee, O Our Father

Author Unknown

Salvatore Ferretti
Arr. by James Turle

1. We thank Thee, O our Fa-ther, For all Thy lov-ing care;
2. Out in the sun-ny mead-ows And in the wood-lands cool,
3. And in the dust-y cit-y, Where bus-y crowds pass by,
4. And wheth-er in the cit-y Or in the fields they dwell;

We thank Thee that Thou mad-est The world so bright and fair.
Up-on the breez-y hill-side, And by each reed-y pool,
And where the tall dark hous-es Stand up and hide the sky;
Al-ways the same sweet mes-sage The fair, sweet flow-ers tell.

We thank Thee for the sun-shine, And for the pleas-ant showers;
And in the qui-et pas-ture, And by the broad high-way;
And where through lanes and al-leys No pleas-ant breez-es blow,
For they are all so won-drous, They show Thy power a-broad;

And O, our God, we thank Thee, We thank Thee for the flow'rs.
All pure, and fresh, and stain-less, They spring up ev-'ry day.
E'en there, O God, our Fa-ther, Thou mak'st the flow-ers grow.
And they are all so beauteous, They tell Thy love, O God.

Prayer

# Be Thou My Vision

136

Tr. by Mary Byrne
Versified by Eleanor Hull, alt.

Har. by Martin Shaw 1875-1958

1. Be Thou my vi - sion, O Lord of my heart;
2. Be Thou my wis - dom, be Thou my true word;
3. Be Thou my buck - ler, my sword for the fight;
4. Rich - es I heed not, nor man's emp - ty praise;

Naught be all else to me save that Thou art
I ev - er with Thee, and Thou with me, Lord;
Be Thou my dig - ni - ty, Thou my de - light,
Thou mine in - her - i - tance, now and al - ways:

Thou my best thought, by day or by night,
Thou my great Fa - ther, I Thy true son;
Thou my soul's shel - ter, Thou my high tower;
Thou and Thou on - ly; first in my heart,

Wak - ing or sleep - ing, Thy pres - ence my light.
Thou in me dwell - ing, and I with Thee one.
Raise Thou me heaven - ward, O power of my power.
High King of heav - en, my treas - ure Thou art.

Prayer

**137**

# Lord Jesus, Thou Art Mine

Edward Sill

Church Psalter

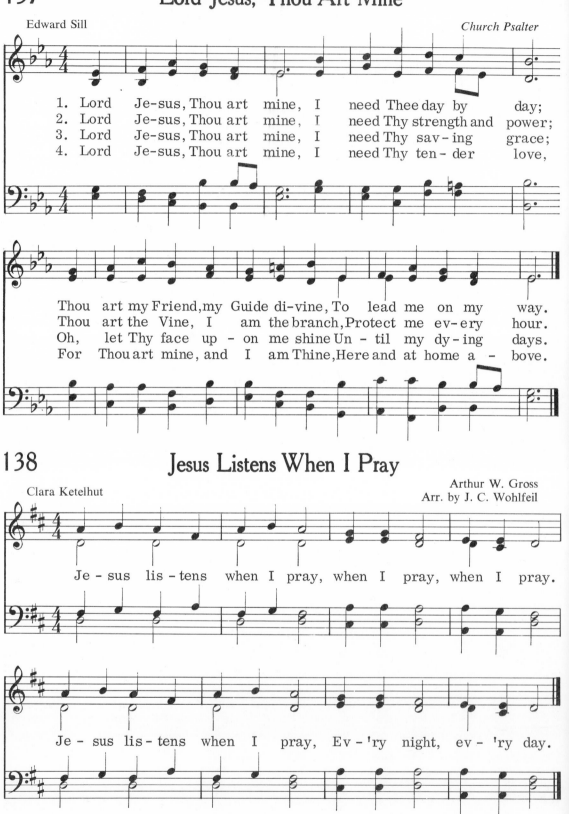

1. Lord Je-sus, Thou art mine, I need Thee day by day;
2. Lord Je-sus, Thou art mine, I need Thy strength and power;
3. Lord Je-sus, Thou art mine, I need Thy sav-ing grace;
4. Lord Je-sus, Thou art mine, I need Thy ten-der love,

Thou art my Friend, my Guide di-vine, To lead me on my way.
Thou art the Vine, I am the branch, Protect me ev-er-y hour.
Oh, let Thy face up-on me shine Un-til my dy-ing days.
For Thou art mine, and I am Thine, Here and at home a - bove.

**138**

# Jesus Listens When I Pray

Arthur W. Gross
Arr. by J. C. Wohlfeil

Clara Ketelhut

Je - sus lis-tens when I pray, when I pray, when I pray.

Je - sus lis-tens when I pray, Ev-'ry night, ev-'ry day.

Prayer

# Savior, Hear Us, We Pray

Author Unknown

Johannes Brahms

1. Sav-ior hear us we pray, Keep us safe thru' this day;
2. Be our Guard-ian and Guide; May we walk by Thy side

Keep our lives free from sin and our hearts pure with-in.
Till the evening shades fall o-ver us, o-ver all.

Je-sus, Lord, hear our prayer, May we rest in Thy care;

Je-sus, Lord, hear our prayer, May we rest in Thy care.

## Wiegenlied

1 Guten Abend, gut' Nacht! mit Rosen bedacht,
mit Näglein besteckt, schlupf unter die Deck.
Morgen früh, wenn Gott will, wirst du wieder geweckt,
morgen früh, wenn Gott will, wirst du wieder geweckt.

2 Guten Abend, gut' Nacht! von Englein bewacht!
Die zeigen im Traum dir Christkindleins Baum.
Schlaf nur selig und süss, schau im Traum's Paradies!
Schlaf nur selig und süss, schau im Traum's Paradies!

Prayer

# The Lord Is Ever Near

Author Unknown

Adapted from *Genevan Psalter*

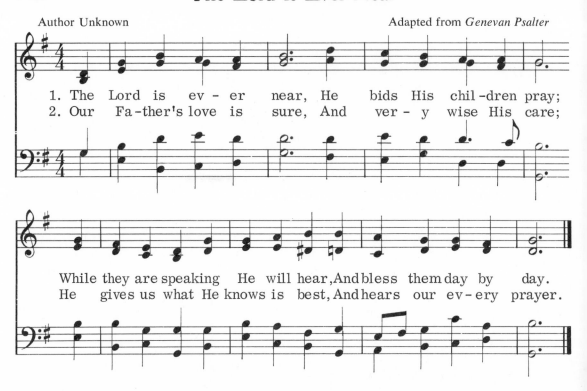

1. The Lord is ev-er near, He bids His chil-dren pray;
2. Our Fa-ther's love is sure, And ver-y wise His care;

While they are speaking He will hear, And bless them day by day.
He gives us what He knows is best, And hears our ev-ery prayer.

141

# Father, We Thank Thee for the Night

Daniel Batchellor

Ascribed to Rebecca J. Weston

Har. by Austin C. Lovelace

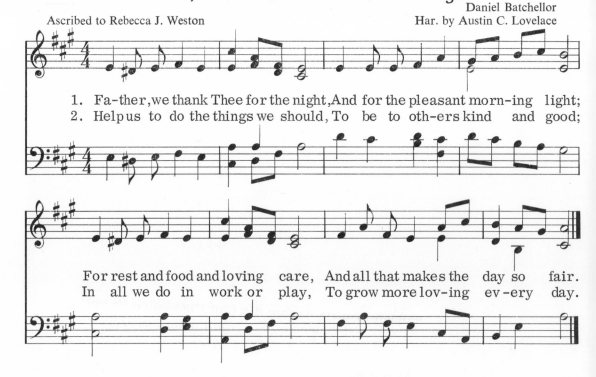

1. Fa-ther, we thank Thee for the night, And for the pleasant morn-ing light;
2. Help us to do the things we should, To be to oth-ers kind and good;

For rest and food and loving care, And all that makes the day so fair.
In all we do in work or play, To grow more lov-ing ev-ery day.

Prayer

# Teach Us to Pray

Author Unknown

Gregorian Chant
Arr. by Lowell Mason

1. O God, whose love en - folds us all,
2. O God, whose help is ev - er near,

Whose boun - ty on - ly waits our call,
Teach us the love that knows no fear,

Teach us, Your chil - dren, how to pray,
That, trust - ing in Your ho - ly might

To seek Your guid - ance day by day.
We live the truth and love the right.

Prayer

**143**

# Jesus, from Thy Throne on High

T. B. Pollock

E. Bunnett
Arr. by Mary Ann Kooker

1. Je - sus, from Thy throne on high, Far a - bove the bright blue sky,
2. Lit - tle chil - dren need not fear, When they know that Thou art near,
3. Lit - tle hearts may love Thee well, Lit - tle lips Thy love may tell;

Look on us with lov - ing eye, Hear us, Ho - ly Je - sus.
Thou dost love us, Sav - ior dear. Hear us, Ho - ly Je - sus.
Lit - tle hymns Thy prais - es swell. Hear us, Ho - ly Je - sus.

**144**

# Thank Thee, Heav'nly Father

Florence Martin

Old French Melody
Arr. by Florence Martin

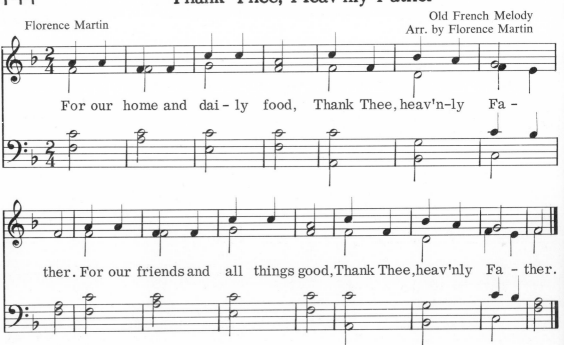

For our home and dai - ly food, Thank Thee, heav'n-ly Fa -

ther. For our friends and all things good, Thank Thee, heav'nly Fa - ther.

Prayer

# Now Thank We the Father

Mary Peacock

Mary Peacock

1. The day is so love-ly, the world is so
2. Now thank we the Fa-ther for ev-'ry good

fair, There's blue in the heav-ens and fall in the
thing, For au-tumn's rich har-vest, for win-ter and

air; There's frost on the mead-ow and gold from the
spring; His love is a-round us, it lives ev-'ry-

sun, Now thank we the Fa-ther for this day be-gun.
where, In days that are love-ly, a world that is fair.

Prayer

# 146 God Is Love

August Rische
Tr. by Lester Hostetler

Thüringer Weise

1. For God so loved us, He sent the Sav - ior;
2. He sent the Sav - ior, The blest Re - deem - er;
3. And I will praise Thee, Thou love im - mor - tal;

For God so loved us, And loves me too.
He sent the Sav - ior To set me free.
And I will praise Thee For ev - er more.

I'll sing it o'er and o'er: The won - drous sto - ry,

That God so loved us, And loves me too.

## Gott ist die Liebe

1 Gott ist die Liebe, lässt mich erlösen;
  Gott ist die Liebe, er liebt auch mich.

Refrain: Drum sag ich noch einmal: Gott ist die Liebe,
  Gott ist die Liebe, er liebt auch mich.

2 Er sandte Jesum, den treuen Heiland;
  er sandte Jesum und macht mich los.

3 Dich will ich preisen, du ew'ge Liebe,
  dich will ich loben, so lang ich bin.

Love and Joy

# Let Us with a Gladsome Mind

147

John Milton

Arr. from a 13th century French Melody

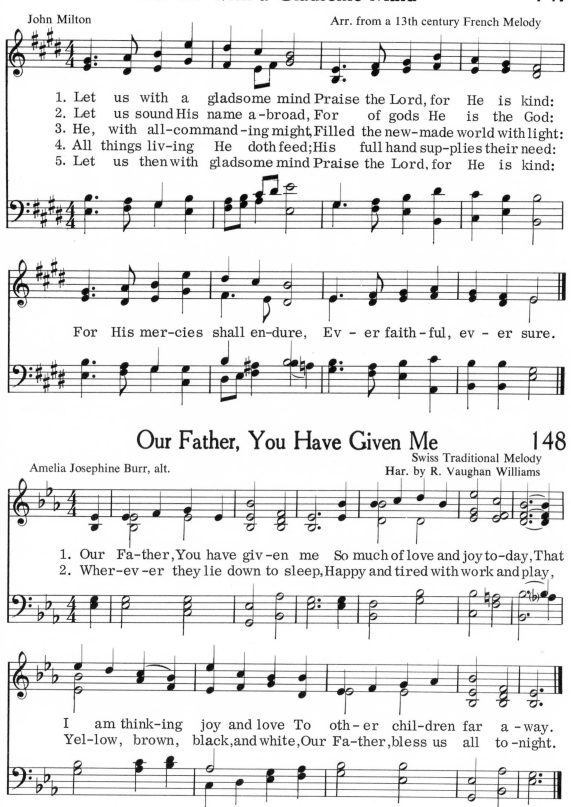

1. Let us with a gladsome mind Praise the Lord, for He is kind:
2. Let us sound His name a-broad, For of gods He is the God:
3. He, with all-command-ing might, Filled the new-made world with light:
4. All things liv-ing He doth feed; His full hand sup-plies their need:
5. Let us then with gladsome mind Praise the Lord, for He is kind:

For His mer-cies shall en-dure, Ev - er faith-ful, ev - er sure.

# Our Father, You Have Given Me

148

Amelia Josephine Burr, alt.

Swiss Traditional Melody
Har. by R. Vaughan Williams

1. Our Fa-ther, You have giv-en me So much of love and joy to-day, That
2. Wher-ev-er they lie down to sleep, Happy and tired with work and play,

I am think-ing joy and love To oth-er chil-dren far a-way.
Yel-low, brown, black, and white, Our Fa-ther, bless us all to-night.

Love and Joy

Our Beautiful Earth

Frances E. Jacobs                                        German Folk Song

How beau-ti-ful is the green earth, The stars in the heav-en a-

bove! But what would the whole world be worth If we

did not fill it with love, with love, If we did not fill it with love?

150 Alleluia Round

Al - le - lu - ia, Al - le - lu - ia, Al - le - lu - ia.

Love and Joy

## Mother's Day

151

Jeana A. Graham

Katherine Y. Guess

1. When Je - sus was a child He knew A moth-er's lov - ing care; We ask His spe - cial bless - ing now For moth-ers liv - ing ev - 'ry-where.

2. A moth - er's hands are quick and strong, Yet gen - tle as can be; There is no task too big or small That they won't do for you and me.

3. Al - though we choose a spe - cial day To show our love is true; One day is not e - nough to prove The love we feel the whole year through.

From *Cherub Hymns*.   Reprinted by permission of Harold Flammer, Inc.

The Christian Home

**152**            Homes

Mary Ambler Marshall            Melody from the *Hirschberg Gesangbuch*

1. Some homes are on the moun-tain - side, And some where riv-ers flow, And some where flow-ers bloom, and some In lands of ice and snow; It does not real-ly mat-ter where, If gen-tle hearts and love are there.

2. I like to think of chil-dren's homes, Wher-ev - er they may be, On hill or plain, in bus-y town, Or by the lone-ly sea; A - round the wide world ev - ery-where All homes are in God's lov-ing care!

The Christian Home

# Once Again Has Come My Birthday

Author Unknown

John Stainer

Once a-gain has come my birth-day, Hap-py time, I'm glad 'tis here;

Now a lov-ing gift for Je-sus, He has kept me one more year.

# To Thy Father and Thy Mother

Corner's *Gesangbuch*
Arr. by Paul G. Bunjes

Anne Ross Cousin, alt.

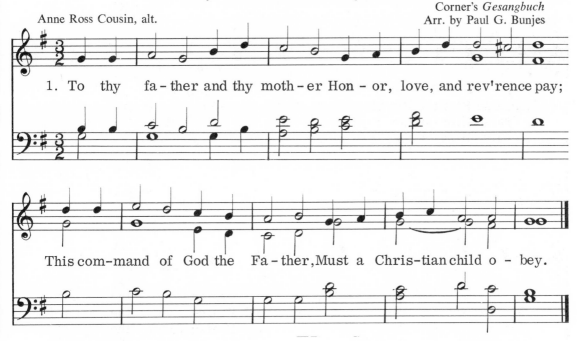

1. To thy fa-ther and thy moth-er Hon-or, love, and rev'rence pay;

This com-mand of God the Fa-ther, Must a Chris-tian child o-bey.

2 Jesus Christ, my Lord, fulfilled it
In His home at Nazareth__
So His heavenly Father willed it __
While a child He lived on earth.

3 Help me, Lord, in this my duty;
Guide me in Thy steps divine;
Show me all the joy and beauty
Of obedience such as Thine.

The Christian Home

## 155 This Is the Day the Lord Hath Made

Isaac Watts

Johann Crüger

1. This is the day the Lord hath made; He calls the hours His own.
2. Ho - san - na in the high-est strains The church on earth can raise;

Let heaven rejoice, let earth be glad, And praise sur-round the throne.
The high-est heavens, in which He reigns, Shall give Him no - bler praise.

## 156 Praise the Lord

Charles Edward Pollock

Charles Edward Pollock
Arr. by James W. Bixel

1. Lit - tle chil - dren, praise the Lord, Praise the Lord, praise the Lord,
2. Praise Him for His bless - ed Word, Bless - ed Word, bless - ed Word,
3. Praise Him for the Sab - bath day, Sab - bath day, Sab - bath day,
4. Praise Him for the Sun - day school, Sun - day school, Sun - day school,

Lit - tle chil - dren, praise the Lord, Praise ye the Lord.
Praise Him for His bless - ed Word, Praise ye the Lord.
Praise Him for the Sab - bath day, Praise ye the Lord.
Praise Him for the Sun - day school, Praise ye the Lord.

The Lord's Day

# Sunday Morning Song

157

Joseph W. Clokey, alt.

Joseph W. Clokey

I be-lieve that on this day I should go to church to pray,

Pray to Je-sus Christ, my Lord, And to hear His ho-ly Word.

# Father, Bless Our School Today

158

Author Unknown

Freylinghausen's *Gesangbuch*

1. Fa - ther, bless our school to - day; Be in all we do or say;
2. Je - sus, well - be - lov - ed Son, May Thy will by us be done;
3. Ho - ly Spir - it, Teach - er, Friend, Grace and blessings on us send;
4. Ho - ly Fa - ther, Ho - ly Son, Ho - ly Spir - it, Three in One!

Be in ev - 'ry song we sing, Ev - 'ry prayer to Thee we bring.
Come and meet with us to - day; Teach us, Lord, thy - self we pray.
Un - to us Thy pow - er give; Touch our souls that we may live.
Glo - ry as of old to Thee Now and ev - er - more shall be.

The Lord's Day

# Lord, This Day Thy Children Meet

William Walsham How

Justin Heinrich Knecht

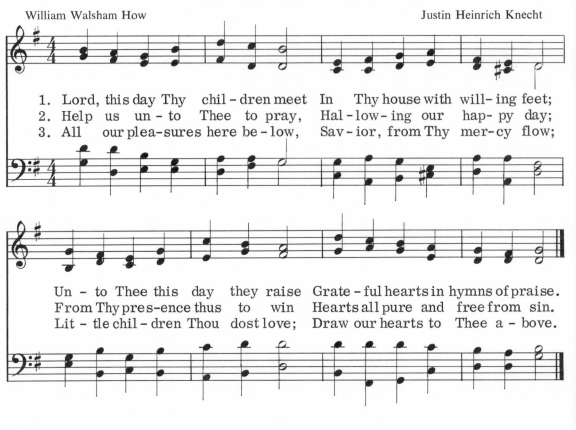

1. Lord, this day Thy chil-dren meet In Thy house with will-ing feet;
2. Help us un-to Thee to pray, Hal-low-ing our hap-py day;
3. All our plea-sures here be-low, Sav-ior, from Thy mer-cy flow;

Un-to Thee this day they raise Grate-ful hearts in hymns of praise.
From Thy pres-ence thus to win Hearts all pure and free from sin.
Lit-tle chil-dren Thou dost love; Draw our hearts to Thee a-bove.

# This Is God's House

Louise M. Oglevee

W. G. Oglevee

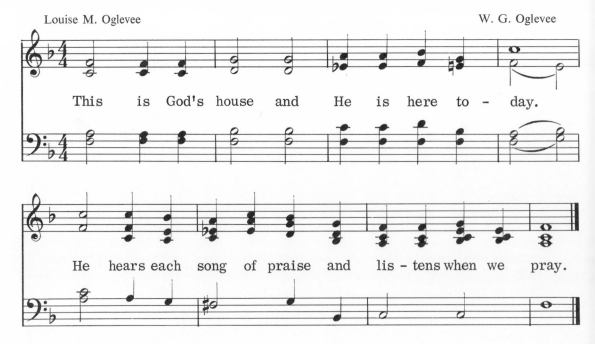

This is God's house and He is here to-day.

He hears each song of praise and lis-tens when we pray.

The Lord's Day

# The Christian Year

Katherine Hankey, alt.

Traditional Melody

1. Ad-vent tells us Christ is near; Christ-mas tells us Christ is here.

In E-pi-pha-ny we trace All the glo-ry of His grace.

2 Then three Sundays will prepare
For the time of fast and prayer,
That, with hearts made penitent,
We may keep a faithful Lent.

3 Holy Week and Easter then
Tell who died and rose again:
O that happy Easter Day!
"Christ is ris'n indeed," we say.

4 Yes, and Christ ascended, too,
To prepare a place for you;
So we give Him special praise
After those great forty days.

5 Then He sent the Holy Ghost
On the day of Pentecost,
With us ever to abide:
Well may we keep Whitsuntide.

6 Last of all, we humbly sing
Glory to our God and King,
Glory to the One in Three,
On the Feast of Trinity.

The Christian Year

**162**

# When Morning Gilds the Skies

From the German
Tr. by Edward Caswall

Joseph Barnby

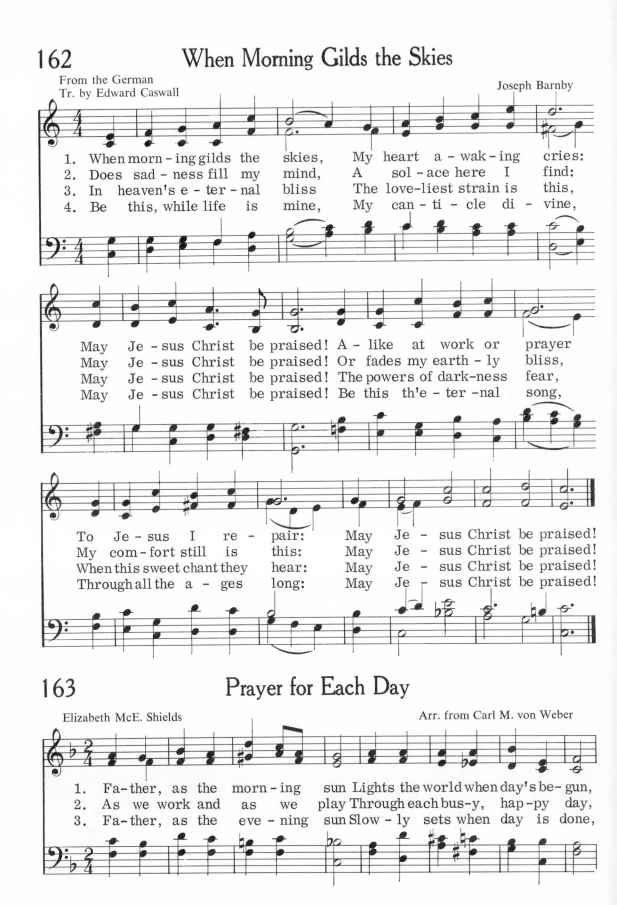

1. When morn-ing gilds the skies, My heart a-wak-ing cries:
2. Does sad-ness fill my mind, A sol-ace here I find:
3. In heaven's e-ter-nal bliss The love-liest strain is this,
4. Be this, while life is mine, My can-ti-cle di-vine,

May Je-sus Christ be praised! A-like at work or prayer
May Je-sus Christ be praised! Or fades my earth-ly bliss,
May Je-sus Christ be praised! The powers of dark-ness fear,
May Je-sus Christ be praised! Be this th'e-ter-nal song,

To Je-sus I re-pair: May Je-sus Christ be praised!
My com-fort still is this: May Je-sus Christ be praised!
When this sweet chant they hear: May Je-sus Christ be praised!
Through all the a-ges long: May Je-sus Christ be praised!

**163**

# Prayer for Each Day

Elizabeth McE. Shields

Arr. from Carl M. von Weber

1. Fa-ther, as the morn-ing sun Lights the world when day's be-gun,
2. As we work and as we play Through each bus-y, hap-py day,
3. Fa-ther, as the eve-ning sun Slow-ly sets when day is done,

Morning Songs

May our hearts and voic - es pray, "Thank You, God, for this good day."
Fa - ther, help us all to be Strong and brave and true like Thee.
May we rest and feel Thy care Guard-ing chil-dren ev-'ry-where.

## Thanks to God 164

From the Portuguese by
Antonio de Campos Goncalves

Brazilian Folk Song

1. In the morn - ning when I wa - ken, As I
2. When at night the stars are shin - ing, Man - y

kneel and make my prayer, I give thanks to God, the
chil - dren far and near, Talk with God and ask His

Fa - ther, For His ten - der love and care.
bless - ing, Sleep in peace and know no fear.

Morning Songs

**165**

# Dear Lord Jesus, Hear My Prayer

Charles Wesley, alt.

Martin Shaw

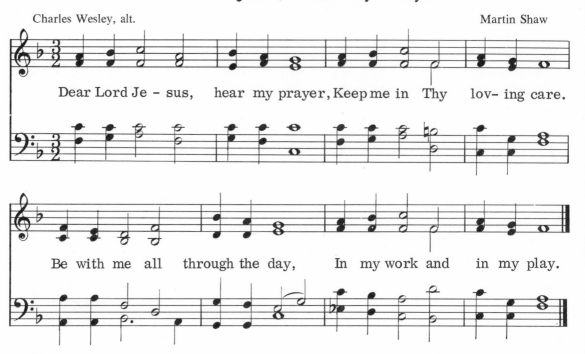

Dear Lord Je - sus, hear my prayer, Keep me in Thy lov- ing care.

Be with me all through the day, In my work and in my play.

**166**

# Children's Chorale

Mary J. Garland

Philip Nicolai

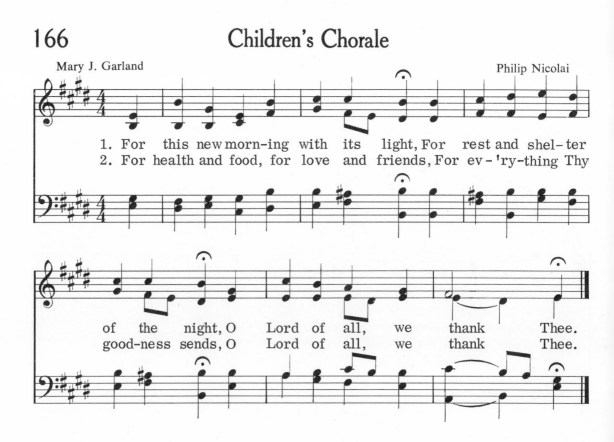

1. For this new morn-ing with its light, For rest and shel-ter
2. For health and food, for love and friends, For ev - 'ry-thing Thy

of the night, O Lord of all, we thank Thee.
good-ness sends, O Lord of all, we thank Thee.

**Morning Songs**

# Now I Wake

*New England Primer*, adapted

From Robert Schumann

Now I wake and see the light;

God has kept me through the night;

I will lift my eyes and pray:

Keep me, Fa - ther, through the day.

Morning Songs

## 168     Thou Who Once on Mother's Knee

F. T. Palgrave

Johann G. Ebeling
Arr. by Paul G. Bunjes

1. Thou who once on moth-er's knee Wast a lit-tle child like me,
2. Be be-side me in the light, Be close by me through the night;

When I wake or go to bed, Lay Thy hands up-on my head;
Make me gen-tle, kind, and true, Do what I am bid to do;

Let me feel Thee ver-y near, Je-sus Christ, my Sav-ior dear.
Help and cheer me when I fret, And for-give when I for-get.

Evening Songs

# My Savior, Hear My Prayer

169

E. C. W.

Henry L. Jenner

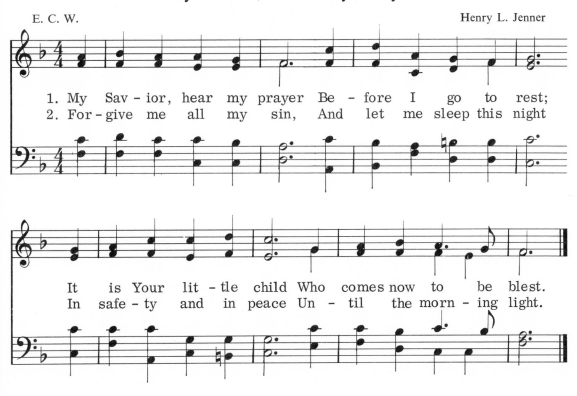

1. My Sav-ior, hear my prayer Be - fore I go to rest;
2. For-give me all my sin, And let me sleep this night

It is Your lit - tle child Who comes now to be blest.
In safe - ty and in peace Un - til the morn - ing light.

# An Evening Hymn

170

Thomas Ken

Thomas Tallis

All praise to Thee, my God, this night, For

all the bless-ings of the light! Keep me, O keep me,

King of kings, Be - neath Thy own al - might - y wings!

Evening Songs

## 171      Jesus, Tender Shepherd, Hear Me

Mary L. Duncan

John Stainer

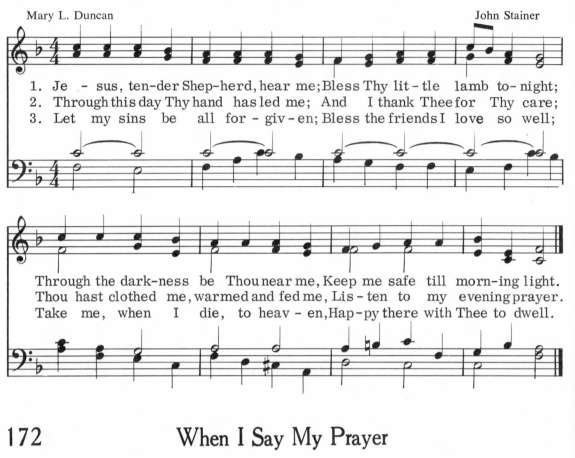

1. Je - sus, ten-der Shep-herd, hear me; Bless Thy lit - tle lamb to-night;
2. Through this day Thy hand has led me; And I thank Thee for Thy care;
3. Let my sins be all for - giv - en; Bless the friends I love so well;

Through the dark-ness be Thou near me, Keep me safe till morn-ing light.
Thou hast clothed me, warmed and fed me, Lis - ten to my evening prayer.
Take me, when I die, to heav - en, Hap-py there with Thee to dwell.

## 172      When I Say My Prayer

Roberta L. Best

Roberta L. Best

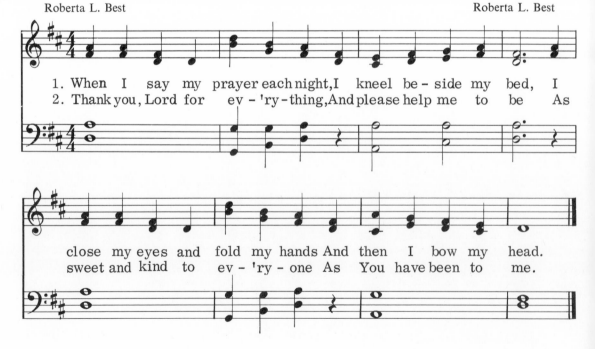

1. When I say my prayer each night, I kneel be - side my bed, I
2. Thank you, Lord for ev - 'ry-thing, And please help me to be As

close my eyes and fold my hands And then I bow my head.
sweet and kind to ev - 'ry - one As You have been to me.

Evening Songs

# Weary, Now I Close Mine Eyes

Luise Hensel
Tr. by Lester Hostetler

Kaiserswerth, 1842

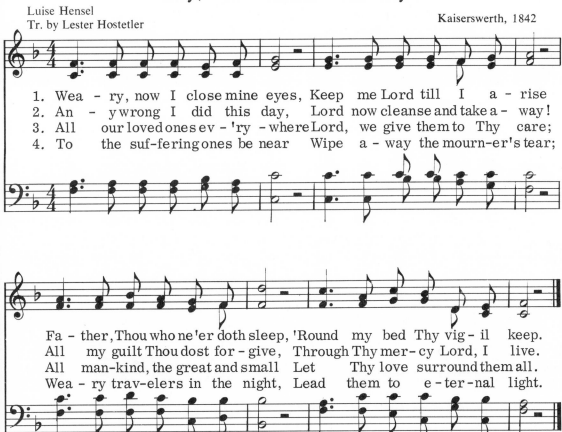

1. Wea - ry, now I close mine eyes, Keep me Lord till I a - rise
2. An - y wrong I did this day, Lord now cleanse and take a - way!
3. All our loved ones ev - 'ry - where Lord, we give them to Thy care;
4. To the suf-fering ones be near Wipe a - way the mourn-er's tear;

Fa - ther, Thou who ne'er doth sleep, 'Round my bed Thy vig - il keep.
All my guilt Thou dost for - give, Through Thy mer - cy Lord, I live.
All man-kind, the great and small Let Thy love surround them all.
Wea - ry trav-elers in the night, Lead them to e - ter-nal light.

## Müde bin ich, geh zur Ruh

1 Müde bin ich, geh zur Ruh,
schliesse meine Augen zu;
Vater, lass die Augen dein
über meinem Bette sein.

2 Hab ich Unrecht heut getan,
sieh es, treuer Gott, nicht an!
Deine Gnad und Jesu Blut
macht ja allen Schaden gut.

3 Alle, die mir sind verwandt,
Gott, lass ruhn in deiner Hand;
alle Menschen, gross und klein,
sollen dir befohlen sein.

4 Kranken Herzen sende Ruh,
nasse Augen schliesse zu;
lass, die noch im Finstern gehn,
bald den Stern der Weisen sehn!

Evening Songs

**174** ## Sing to the Lord of Harvest

J. S. B. Monsell

*Himmlische Harpffe Davids*

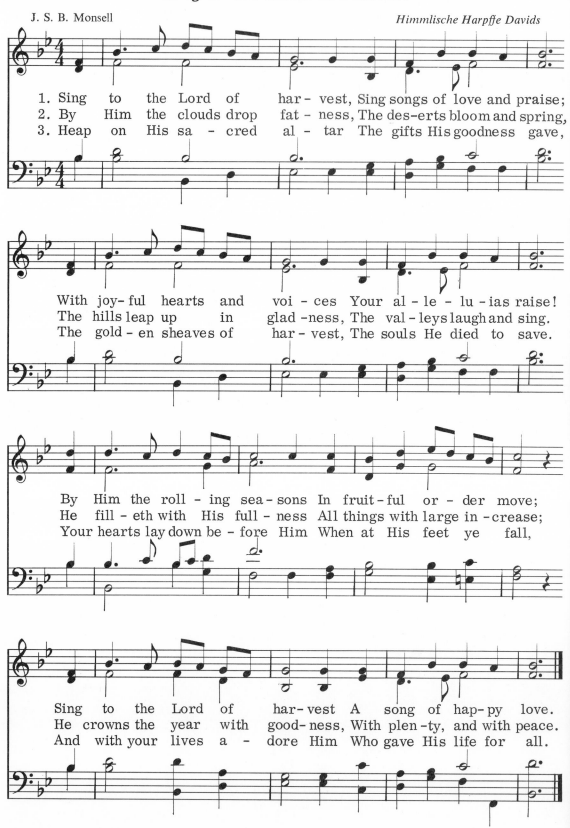

1. Sing to the Lord of har - vest, Sing songs of love and praise;
2. By Him the clouds drop fat - ness, The des-erts bloom and spring,
3. Heap on His sa - cred al - tar The gifts His goodness gave,

With joy-ful hearts and voi - ces Your al - le - lu -ias raise!
The hills leap up in glad -ness, The val -leys laugh and sing.
The gold - en sheaves of har - vest, The souls He died to save.

By Him the roll - ing sea-sons In fruit-ful or - der move;
He fill - eth with His full - ness All things with large in -crease;
Your hearts lay down be - fore Him When at His feet ye fall,

Sing to the Lord of har-vest A song of hap-py love.
He crowns the year with good-ness, With plen -ty, and with peace.
And with your lives a - dore Him Who gave His life for all.

**Harvest and Thanksgiving**

# Praise to God, Immortal Praise

Anna L. Barbauld

Asahel Abbot

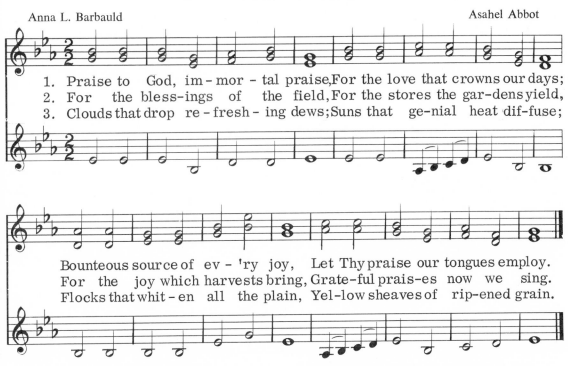

1. Praise to God, im - mor - tal praise, For the love that crowns our days;
2. For the bless-ings of the field, For the stores the gar-dens yield,
3. Clouds that drop re - fresh - ing dews; Suns that ge-nial heat dif-fuse;

Bounteous source of ev - 'ry joy, Let Thy praise our tongues employ.
For the joy which harvests bring, Grate-ful prais-es now we sing.
Flocks that whit - en all the plain, Yel-low sheaves of rip-ened grain.

4 All that spring with bounteous hand,
Scatters o'er the smiling land;
All that lib'ral autumn pours
From her overflowing stores;

5 These, great God, to Thee we owe,
Source whence all our blessings flow;
And for these our souls shall raise
Grateful vows and solemn praise.

# Thanksgiving Time Has Come

Old Folk Song

Author Unknown

Arr. by Evelyn Bushong

Thanks-giv-ing time has come a-gain, Thank our lov-ing Fa - ther;

Thank Him, Thank Him, Thank Him, Thank Him; Thank Him for our* _____

*The children may suggest things for which they wish to thank God.

Harvest and Thanksgiving

**177**

# When the Corn Is Planted

Author Unknown

Timothy Richard Matthews

1. When the corn is plant-ed     In the deep dark bed,
2. God sends sun and show-ers,    Birds sing o-ver-head,
3. When the corn is gath-ered,    Stored in barn and shed,
4. Fa-ther high in heav-en,       All by Thee are fed;

Moth-ers know their chil-dren   Will have dai-ly bread.
While the corn is grow-ing      For our dai-ly bread.
Then we all are thank-ful       For our dai-ly bread.
Hear Thy chil-dren praise Thee  For our dai-ly bread.

**178**

# God Hath Given Us Harvest

J. A. Davies

Joh. Christoph Heinrich Rinck

1. God hath giv'n us har-vest,   Let us praise His name;
2. Year by year His prom-ise      Faith-ful-ly en-dures;
3. Rain from heav'n He send-eth    On the grow-ing grain;
4. Glo-ry, then, for-ev-er         Be to Fa-ther, Son,

While the earth re-main-eth,     He is still the same.
Seed-time, sun-shine, har-vest,  He for men in-sures.
Fruit-ful sea-sons gives us;     Good-ness is His name.
With the Ho-ly Spir-it,          Bless-ed Three in One.

Harvest and Thanksgiving

# Come, Ye Thankful People, Come

Henry Alford

George J. Elvey

1. Come, ye thank - ful peo - ple, come, Raise the song of har-vest home:
2. All     the world is God's own field, Fruit un - to His praise to yield;

All     is safe - ly gath-ered in, Ere the win -ter storms be-gin;
Wheat and tares to - geth-er sown, Un - to joy or sor-row grown:

God, our Mak - er, doth pro - vide For our wants to    be sup-plied:
First the blade, and  then the   ear, Then the full corn shall ap - pear:

Come    to God's own tem - ple, come, Raise the song of har-vest home.
Lord    of har - vest, grant that we    Wholesome grain and pure may   be.

Harvest and Thanksgiving

# 180 Winter Song

Somerset Folk Song

1. A - bove the world the win-ter stars, The love-ly stars, look down
2. A - cross the dark the win-ter dawn Comes slow-ly up the sky,

On snow-y wood and si-lent hill, On road and field and town
Fair col-ors spread-ing north and south, Like ban-ners lift-ed high.

So clear and far, so calm and bright, God's glo-ry in the night.
O rose and gold and red un-furled A-bove God's love-ly world!

The Seasons

# Millions of Snowflakes

Mary Royer

Mary Royer
Arr. by J. Harold Moyer

Mil-lions of snowflakes are cov'ring the ground, Soft - ly, soft-ly. Their

wool - ly white blanket is tucked all around, Gen - tly, gen-tly. From the

cold win-ter sky to the earth far be-low The Fa-ther has sent us the

gift of the snow. Oh, He giv - eth snow like wool!

The Seasons

# Lo, the Winter Is Past

Song of Solomon 2:11, 12

Edward Shippen Barnes

Lo, the win-ter is past; The rain is o-ver and gone;

The flowers appear on the earth; The time of the sing-ing of birds is come.

**The Seasons**

# Autumn

**183**

Ida F. Leyda

Helen M. Browne
Arr. by Evelyn Bushong

1. Ap - ples mel - low, Pump-kins yel - low, Tell the time of year;
2. Col - ors gai - ly Chang-ing dai - ly, Bright-en field and wood;

Nuts are fall - ing, Na - ture call - ing, Au - tumn time is here.
Au - tumn's glo - ry Tells the sto - ry, God is great and good.

# Song of the Seasons

**184**

Aurora M. Shumate

Ida T. Truss

1. The win - ter has gone, The spring-time is here;
2. The spring-time has gone, The sum - mer is here;
3. The sum - mer has gone, The au - tumn is here;
4. The au - tumn has gone, The win - ter is here;

And ev - 'ry - thing tells me God is near.
And ev - 'ry - thing tells me God is near.
And ev - 'ry - thing tells me God is near.
And ev - 'ry - thing tells me God is near.

The Seasons

On Children's Day We Sweetly Sing

Margaret L. Williams

English Traditional Melody
Arr. by R. Vaughan Williams

1. On Chil-dren's Day we sweetly sing To tell our Father's care,
2. The flow-ers bloom, the birds do sing, All crea-tures praise the Lord,

And join in grate-ful praise of Him With chil-dren ev-'ry-where.
And with all na-ture chil-dren raise Their song in glad ac-cord.

Though boys and girls of oth-er lands In oth-er lan-guage sing,
As by God's sun the flow-ers bloom, And by His care birds sing,

We share with them our songs of joy And hail the children's King.
So by His grace we chil-dren live: Give thanks to God our King.

Children's Day

# "Hosanna!" Be the Children's Song

James Montgomery
Stanza 1, line 3, alt.

*Gesangbuch der Herzogl.*
*Wirtembergischen Katholischen Hofkapelle*

1. "Ho - san - na!" be the chil-dren's song To Christ, the children's King;
2. "Ho - san - na!" sound from hill to hill, And spread from plain to plain;

His praise, to whom they all be-long, Let all the chil-dren sing.
While, loud-er, sweet-er, clear-er still, Woods ech-o to the strain.

"Ho - san - na!" then, our song shall be; "Ho - san - na to our King!"

This is the chil-dren's ju - bi - lee; Let all the chil-dren sing.

Children's Day

**187**

# God Himself Is with Us

Gerhard Tersteegen

Neander's *Bundes-Lieder*
Arr. by J. Harold Moyer

God him-self is with us: Let us now a-dore Him, And with awe ap-

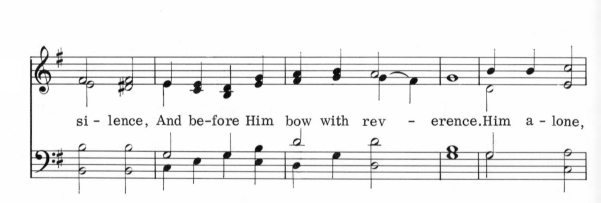

pear be-fore Him. God is in His tem-ple, All with-in keep

si - lence, And be-fore Him bow with rev - erence. Him a - lone,

God we own; To our Lord and Sav - ior Prais-es sing for-ev - er.

Calls to Worship

# O Come, Let Us Worship

Psalm 95:6

Kyrie by George J. Elvey
Arr. by Edward Shippen Barnes

O come, let us wor - ship and bow down: Let us kneel be - fore the Lord our Mak - er.

# O Worship the Lord

Psalm 96:9; 136:1

Walter E. Yoder

O wor - ship the Lord, In the beau - ty of ho - li - ness O give thanks un - to the Lord, For He is good.

Calls to Worship

**190**

# Let All Mortal Flesh Keep Silence

Liturgy of St. James
Tr. by Gerard Moultrie

French Traditional Carol

Let all mor-tal flesh keep si - lence, And with fear and

trem - bling stand; Pon - der noth-ing earth - ly mind - ed,

For with bless-ing in His hand, Christ our God to earth de-

scend — eth, Our full hom-age to de - mand.

Calls to Worship

# O Come and Let Us Worship

## 191

Adapted from refrain of Latin Hymn, 17th century
Tr. by Frederick Oakeley

Wade's *Cantus Diversi*

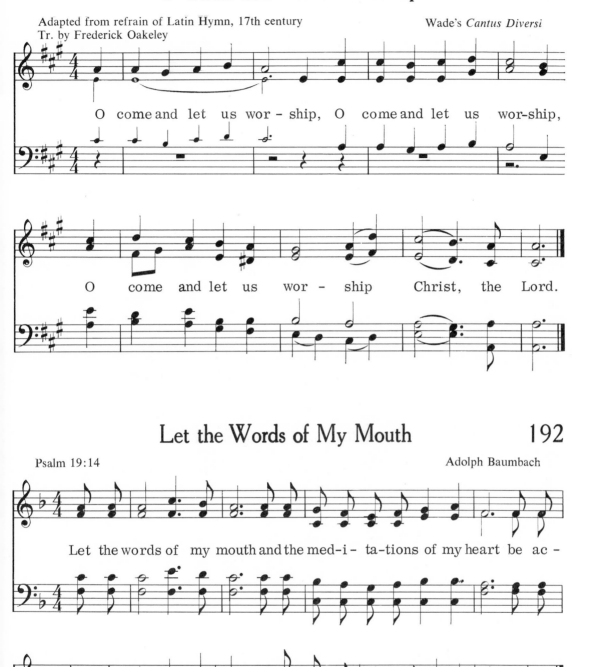

O come and let us wor-ship, O come and let us wor-ship,

O come and let us wor - ship Christ, the Lord.

# Let the Words of My Mouth

## 192

Psalm 19:14

Adolph Baumbach

Let the words of my mouth and the med-i- ta-tions of my heart be ac -

cept - a -ble in Thy sight, O Lord, my Strength and my Re-deem-er.

Calls to Worship

## 193     Here We Come with Gladness

Julia H. Johnston

Music from *Kleiner Liederschatz*

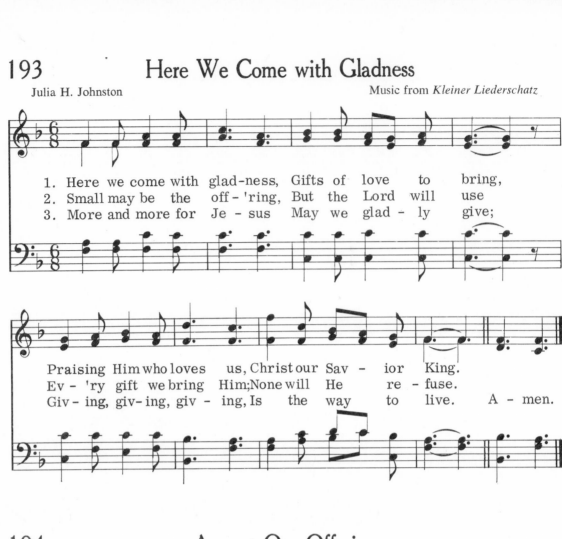

1. Here we come with glad-ness, Gifts of love to bring,
2. Small may be the off-'ring, But the Lord will use
3. More and more for Je-sus May we glad-ly give;

Praising Him who loves us, Christ our Sav - ior King.
Ev - 'ry gift we bring Him; None will He re - fuse.
Giv - ing, giv-ing, giv - ing, Is the way to live. A - men.

## 194     Accept Our Offering

Elizabeth A. Showalter

Arr. from William V. Wallace

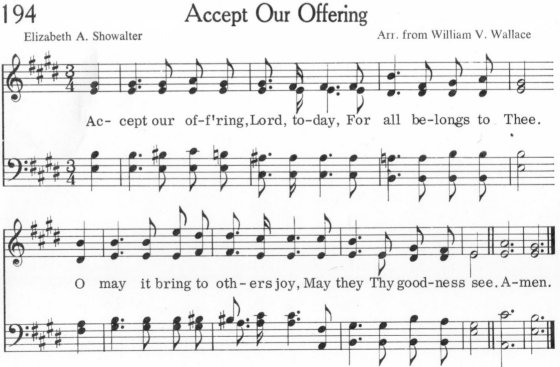

Ac- cept our of-f'ring, Lord, to-day, For all be-longs to Thee.

O may it bring to oth-ers joy, May they Thy good-ness see. A-men.

Offertory Songs

# We Give Thee But Thine Own
## 195

William Walsham How

Arr. from Robert Schumann

1. We give Thee but Thine own, What-e'er the gift may be;
2. May we Thy boun-ties thus As stewards true re-ceive,
3. To com-fort and to bless, To find a balm for woe,
4. And we be-lieve Thy word, Though dim our faith may be;

All that we have is Thine a-lone, A trust, O Lord, from Thee.
And glad-ly, as Thou bless-est us, To Thee our first fruits give.
To tend the lone and fa-ther-less Is Christlike work be-low.
What-e'er for Thine we do, O Lord, We do it un-to Thee. A-men.

# Thy Work, O God, Needs Many Hands
## 196

Calvin W. Laufer

John H. Gower

1. Thy work, O God, needs man-y hands To help Thee ev-'ry-where,
2. Be-cause we love Thee and Thy work, Our of-fering now we make;

And some there are who can-not serve Unless our gifts we share.
Be pleased to use it as Thine own, We ask for Je-sus' sake. A-men.

**197**

# All Good Gifts Around Us

Matthias Claudius
Tr. by Jane M. Campbell

Johann A. P. Schulz

All good gifts a-round us Are sent from heaven a-bove;

Then thank the Lord, O thank the Lord For all His love. A-men.

**198**

# Kum Ba Yah

Author Unknown

African

1. Kum ba yah, my Lord, Kum ba yah! Kum ba yah! My, Lord, Kum ba yah!
2. Someone's crying, Lord, Kum ba yah! Someone's crying, Lord, Kum ba yah!
3. Someone's singing, Lord, Kum ba yah! Someone's singing, Lord, Kum ba yah!
4. Someone's praying, Lord, Kum ba yah! Someone's praying, Lord, Kum ba yah!

Kum ba yah, my Lord, Kum ba yah! Oh, Lord, Kum ba yah!
Someone's cry-ing, Lord, Kum ba yah! Oh, Lord, Kum ba yah!
Someone's sing-ing, Lord, Kum ba yah! Oh, Lord, Kum ba yah!
Someone's pray-ing, Lord, Kum ba yah! Oh, Lord, Kum ba yah!

General Prayers

# Can a Growing Child Like Me?

199

Attributed to Mary Mapes Dodge

W. K. Basswood
Arr. by Ellen Jane Lorenz

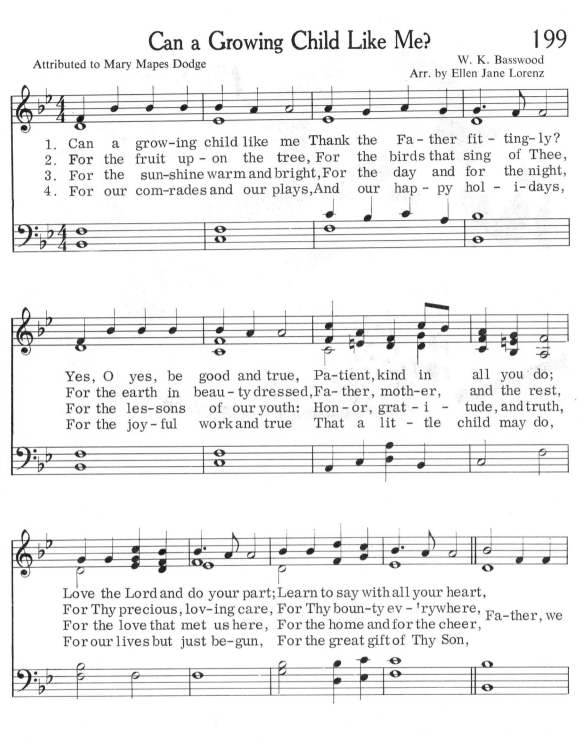

1. Can a grow-ing child like me Thank the Fa-ther fit-ting-ly?
2. For the fruit up-on the tree, For the birds that sing of Thee,
3. For the sun-shine warm and bright, For the day and for the night,
4. For our com-rades and our plays, And our hap-py hol-i-days,

Yes, O yes, be good and true, Pa-tient, kind in all you do;
For the earth in beau-ty dressed, Fa-ther, moth-er, and the rest,
For the les-sons of our youth: Hon-or, grat-i-tude, and truth,
For the joy-ful work and true That a lit-tle child may do,

Love the Lord and do your part; Learn to say with all your heart,
For Thy precious, lov-ing care, For Thy boun-ty ev-'rywhere,
For the love that met us here, For the home and for the cheer, Fa-ther, we
For our lives but just be-gun, For the great gift of Thy Son,

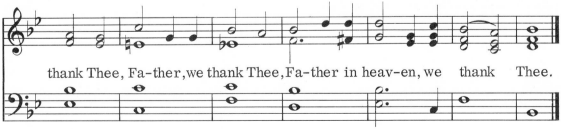

thank Thee, Fa-ther, we thank Thee, Fa-ther in heav-en, we thank Thee.

Harmonization copyright 1957 by Otterbein Press, used by permission.

General Prayers

## 200        Hear Our Prayer, O Lord

Author Unknown

George Whelpton

Hear our prayer, O Lord,     Hear our prayer, O Lord;

In - cline Thine ear to us, And grant us Thy peace.    A - men.

General Prayers

# Thanking God

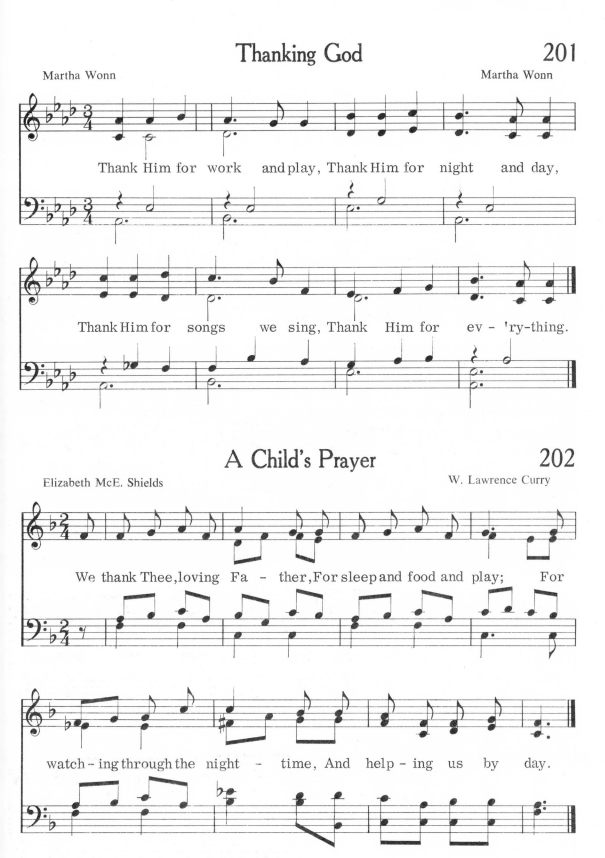

Martha Wonn

Martha Wonn

Thank Him for work and play, Thank Him for night and day,

Thank Him for songs we sing, Thank Him for ev-'ry-thing.

# A Child's Prayer

Elizabeth McE. Shields

W. Lawrence Curry

We thank Thee, loving Fa-ther, For sleep and food and play;

watch-ing through the night-time, And help-ing us by day.

General Prayers

## 203 Lord, Who Lovest All Thy Children

Mira Rowland, alt.

Adapted from Novello

1. Lord, who lov - est all Thy chil - dren,
2. Thou who lived a ho - ly child life,
3. In our school - time and our play - ing,

Hear us as we pray to Thee.
Help us to be pure like Thee.
Make us gen - tle, Lord, like Thee.

4. Thou didst live Thy life for others,
   Make us helpful, Lord, like Thee.

5. Thou on earth wast ever loving,
   Make us ever more like Thee.

## 204 Forgive Me, God

An Episcopal Church School Class

Alt. from *The Revivalist*

For - give me, God, for things I've done That were not kind and good,

For - give me, God, and help me try To do the things I should.

General Prayers

# Spirit of the Living God

Daniel Iverson

Daniel Iverson

Spir - it of the liv - ing God, Now de-scend on me!

Spir - it of the liv-ing God, Now de-scend on me!

Break me, melt me, Mold me, fill me!

Spir - it of the liv-ing God, Now de-scend on me!

General Prayers

206      **Thank You, Loving Father**

Arthur W. Gross

Ernestine Huber
Arr. by Theo. J. Koch

1. God made all the food    we   eat; Thank You, lov-ing Fa - ther.
2. God made all the birds   that sing; Thank You, lov-ing Fa - ther.

God made all the flow'rs so sweet; Thank You, lov-ing Fa - ther.
God made us and ev - 'ry-thing; Thank You, lov-ing Fa - ther.

General Prayers

# Savior, Again to Thy Dear Name

John Ellerton

Edward J. Hopkins

1. Sav - ior, a - gain to Thy dear name we raise
2. Grant us Thy peace up - on our home - ward way;

With one ac - cord our part - ing hymn of praise;
With Thee be - gan, with Thee shall end the day:

We stand to bless Thee ere our wor - ship cease;
Guard Thou the lips from sin, the hearts from shame,

Then, low - ly kneel - ing, wait Thy word of peace.
That in this house have call'd up - on Thy name.

Closing Prayers

## 208 Father, We Thank You for Your Word

Ida Boyer Bontrager

*Musikalischer Christenschatz*

Fa-ther, we thank You for Your Word And for the lessons we have heard;

Be with us as we homeward go; Help us do the things we know.

## 209 The Lord Be with Us

John Ellerton

Jeremiah Clark

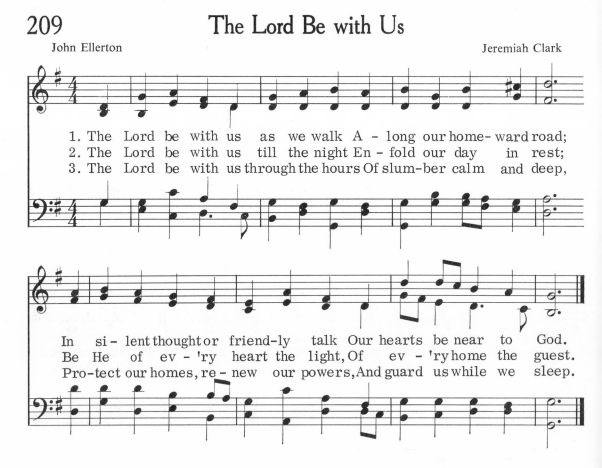

1. The Lord be with us as we walk A - long our home-ward road;
2. The Lord be with us till the night En - fold our day in rest;
3. The Lord be with us through the hours Of slum-ber calm and deep,

In si - lent thought or friend-ly talk Our hearts be near to God.
Be He of ev - 'ry heart the light, Of ev - 'ry home the guest.
Pro-tect our homes, re - new our powers, And guard us while we sleep.

**Closing Prayers**

# Praise and Thanksgiving Let Everyone Bring

**210**

Paraphrase of the German
Tr. by Edith Lovell Thomas

Alsatian Round
Har. by Derek Ferris

1. Praise and thanks-giv — ing let ev-'ry-one bring
2. Lo - bet und prei — set, ihr Völ - ker den Herrn!

Un - to our Fa — ther for ev-'ry good thing.
Freu - et euch sei — ner und die - net ihm gern.

All to-geth — er joy-ful-ly sing!
All' ihr Völ — ker, lo - bet den Herrn!

By omitting the harmony, the melody may by used as a round.

## Praise We the Father

Praise we the Father, by whom we are fed;
Thank Him for giving us daily our bread.
Praise Him, Praise Him, Praise Him for bread.

To be sung to the above tune
Text by Lester Hostetler.

Table Prayers

**211** Choral Grace

Emilie Fendall Johnson and Eleanor Graham

Johann H. Schein
Arr. by James W. Bixel

We thank Thee, Lord, for hap-py hearts, For rain and sun-ny weath - er. We thank Thee, Lord, for this our food, And that we are to-geth - er. Be with us, Lord, both night and day, And guide us in our work and play.

Table Prayers

## Chinese Grace

T. C. Chao
Tr. by Bliss Wiant

Chinese Folk Tune

1. Ne'er for-get God's dai - ly care: Health and food and clothes to wear.
2. Free- ly we these gifts re - ceive. May we not His Spir - it grieve.

## Praise God from Whom All Blessings Flow    213

Thomas Ken

Louis Bourgeois

Praise God, from whom all bless - ings flow; Praise Him, all

crea - tures here be - low; Praise Him a - bove, ye

heaven- ly host; Praise Fa - ther, Son, and Ho - ly Ghost. A - men.

### TABLE GRACES

Be present at our table, Lord,
Be here and everywhere adored;
These mercies bless and grant that we
May feast in paradise with Thee.

For food and drink and happy days
Accept our gratitude and praise;
In serving others, Lord, may we
Repay in part our debt to Thee.

**Table Prayers**

# Indexes

# Acknowledgments

Ownership of copyrights has been traced and diligent effort made to locate and secure permission for the use of copyrighted material in this book. If copyrighted material has been used without permission, we would appreciate receiving full information so that proper acknowledgment may be made in future printings.

The following have granted us permission to use their material. All rights reserved by the copyright owners.

Abingdon Press
180—from *Picture Story Paper,* used by permission of Nancy Byrd Turner and The Methodist Publishing House.

American Baptist Board of Education and Publication
75—stanza 1 copyright 1942; 76.

American Book Company
34 and 201—from *The American Singer,* Books 2 and 4 by Beattie, Wolverton, Wilson, and Hinga.

American Tract Society
88.

Baker, Elda Flett
100—music.

Baldwin, Josephine L.
109—words from *Services and Songs for Use in the Junior Department.*

Broadman Press
105 and 184—from *Songs We Sing,* copyright 1939.

Chatto and Windus, Ltd.
136—words from *The Poem Book of Gael* by Eleanor Hull.

The Church Pension Fund
25—music, last three measures altered; 111—music.

Concordia Publishing House
18, 78—arrangement, 138, 154—arrangement, 168 —arrangement, 206.

David C. Cook Publishing Company
120 and 156.

The Curtis Publishing Company
145—from *Jack and Jill,* copyright 1948.

J. Curwen and Sons, Ltd.
24, 165—music.

Davis, Robert
47—words used by permission of Derek A. Lee.

Dietz, Emma S.
183—arrangement.

Faith and Life Press
41, 43, 84, 87—owned jointly with Herald Press.

Friendship Press
37, 164, 210—from *The Whole World Singing* by Edith Lovell Thomas, copyright 1950; 148—words.

The H. W. Gray Company
20—melody; 59—copyright 1944; 157—from *Builders,* copyright 1955.

Hedge, Harry Malcome
122—stanza 1 used by permission of Barbara Hedge Eckholt.

Herald Press
73, 85, 87—owned jointly with Faith and Life Press.
107—words, 175, 181, 189, 194.

Independent Press, Ltd.
61—music from *Congregational Praise.*

Iverson, Daniel
205.

Little, Brown and Company
61—words.

Morehouse-Barlow Co., Inc.
111—words.

National Sunday School Union
17—words and harmonization; 21—words; 80— tune; 121.

National Union of Christian Schools
79—tune arrangement.

Oxford University Press
10—words used by permission of the executors of the estate of F. S. Pierpoint and Oxford University Press. 82—tune arrangement. 21—music from *A Student's Hymnal.* 8, 51, 109, 148, and 185—music from *The English Hymnal.* 28, 32, 38, and 66 from *Hymnbook for Children.* 19—music, 95—words, and 136—harmony from *Songs of Praise,* enlarged edition, copyright 1931, renewed 1939. 19—words, 96—music, and 114—words from *Songs of Praise for Boys and Girls.*

# Authors, Translators, and Sources

# Composers and Arrangers

# Alphabetical Index of Tunes

# Topical Index

# Hymns For Age Groups

To help teachers and others using this book, the hymns have been classified by age groups to guide in the selection of hymns which may be used with three age groups. Hymns suitable for kindergarten children are designated by K, for primary children (grades one to three) by P, and for juniors (grades four to six) by J.

## GOD THE FATHER

### His Wonder and Creation

8   A Little Seed Lay Fast Asleep   P
11  All Things Bright and Beautiful   K   P
6   And God Said   K   P
3   Can You Count the Stars   P   J
10  For the Beauty of the Earth   P   J
9   Give to Our God Immortal Praise   J
5   Praise to God for Things We See   P   J
1   Sing to God in Joyful Voice   P   J
2   This Is My Father's World   P   J
4   Who Made the Sky So Bright and Blue   P
7   Who Made the Stars   K   P

### His Might and Power

14  Before the Lord We Bow   P   J
15  Come, Thou Almighty King   P   J
12  I Sing the Mighty Power of God   J
16  O Worship the King, All Glorious Above   P   J
13  The God of Abraham Praise   J

### His Love and Care

24  Gentle Jesus, Meek and Mild   K   P
20  God Is the Loving Father   P   J
26  God Sees the Little Sparrow Fall   K   P
25  God Who Made the Earth   K   P
17  God, Whose Name Is Love   K   P
18  God's a Father Kind and True   K   P
19  I Love God's Tiny Creatures   J
21  I Love to Think That Jesus Saw   P   J
22  Teach Us, Dear Lord, to Pray   P   J
23  The Lord's My Shepherd   P   J

## JESUS CHRIST OUR LORD

### His Advent and Birth

44  As Each Happy Christmas   K   P   J
38  As Joseph Was A-walking   J
35  Away in a Manger   K   P
41  Christ Was Born in Bethlehem   P   J
43  Christmas Bells Ring Out Glad News   K   P   J
30  From Heaven Above to Earth I Come   P   J
34  Jesus, Born in Bethlea   J
29  O Come, All Ye Faithful   K   P   J
42  O Come, Little Children   K   P
27  O Come, O Come Emmanuel   P   J
31  O du fröhliche   J
33  O Little Town of Bethlehem   K   P   J
40  On a Winter Morning   P   J

28  On Jordan's Bank the Baptist's Cry   J
32  Once in Royal David's City   P   J
39  Shepherds Leave the Hillside   K
45  Silent Night! Holy Night!   K   P   J
37  The First Courier   J
47  The Friendly Beasts   K   P
46  We Three Kings of Orient Are   K   P   J
36  We've Been Told a Joyful Thing   P   J

### His Life and Ministry

51  At Work Beside His Father's Bench   P   J
52  Far Away in Old Judea   P   J
54  Lonesome Valley   P   J
55  O Master Workman of the Race   J
48  O Sing a Song of Bethlehem   P   J
53  Once Upon a Hillside   K   P
50  Thy Works of Love   P   J
49  We Would See Jesus   P   J

### His Triumphal Entry

56  All Glory, Laud, and Honor   J
57  Hosanna, Loud Hosanna   J

### His Suffering, Death, and Resurrection

59  An Easter Carol   P
64  At the Dawn of Easter Day   K   P
63  Christ Is Risen   K   P
67  Christ the Lord Is Risen Today; Alleluia!   K   P
66  Come, O Children, Sing to Jesus   K   P
61  Easter Time   P   J
62  Jesus Christ Is Risen Today   P   J
65  Joyful Easter   P   J
58  There Is a Green Hill Far Away   P   J
60  We Welcome Glad Easter   P   J

## THE CHURCH

### God's People

71  Come, Holy Spirit, Come   P   J
70  Faith of Our Fathers, Living Still   P   J
69  Glorious Things of Thee Are Spoken   J
72  Gracious Spirit, Dove Divine   P   J
68  The Church of God Is Everywhere   P   J

### God's House

74  Here in Our Father's House   K   P   J
77  In Our Church We Gladly Sing   K   P
73  I Was Glad   K   P
75  We Love Our Church, O God   P   J
76  When to Church I Go   K

## WORSHIP RESOURCES

*Calls to Worship*

187  God Himself Is with Us  P  J
190  Let All Mortal Flesh Keep Silence  J
192  Let the Words of My Mouth  K  P  J
191  O Come and Let Us Worship  K  P
188  O Come, Let Us Worship  P  J
189  O Worship the Lord  P

*Offertory Songs*

194  Accept Our Offering  J
193  Here We Come with Gladness  K  P
196  Thy Work, O God, Needs Many Hands  P  J
195  We Give Thee But Thine Own  P  J

*General Prayers*

202  A Child's Prayer  K  P
197  All Good Gifts Around Us  K  P  J
199  Can a Growing Child Like Me?  P
204  Forgive Me, God  K  P
200  Hear Our Prayer, O Lord  K  P  J

198  Kum Ba Ya  K  P  J
203  Lord, Who Lovest All Thy Children  K  P
205  Spirit of the Living God  P  J
206  Thank You, Loving Father  K  P
201  Thanking God  K  P

*Closing Prayers*

208  Father, We Thank You for Your Word  K  P
207  Savior, Again to Thy Dear Name  J
209  The Lord Be with Us  P  J

*Table Prayers*

213  Be Present at Our Table Lord  P  J
212  Chinese Grace  P  J
211  Choral Grace  J
213  For Food and Drink and Happy Days  P  J
210  Praise and Thanksgiving Let Everyone Bring
     K  P  J
213  Praise God from Whom All Blessings Flow  P  J
210  Praise We the Father  K  P  J

# First Lines and Titles